The Walter Lynwood Fleming Lectures in Southern History

LOUISIANA STATE UNIVERSITY

A Sphinx on the American Land

The Nineteenth-Century South in Comparative Perspective

PETER KOLCHIN

LOUISIANA STATE UNIVERSITY PRESS **✶** BATON ROUGE

Designer: Barbara Nealy Bourgoyne
Typeface: Galliard
Typesetter: Coghill Composition, Inc.
Printer and binder: Thomson-Shore, Inc.

ISBN 0-8071-2866-X (cloth)

Portions of Chapter 3 were first published in another form in Enrico Dal Lago and Rick
Halpern, eds., *The American South and the Italian Mezzogiorno: Essays in Comparative History*
(2001), reproduced here with permission of Palgrave Macmillan.

The paper in this book meets the guidelines for permanence and durability of the Committee
on Production Guidelines for Book Longevity of the Council on Library Resources. ♾

IN MEMORY OF
HOWARD N. RABINOWITZ
(1942–1998)

CONTENTS

ACKNOWLEDGMENTS

This volume originated in—and is an expansion of—three talks that I presented as the Walter Lynwood Fleming Lectures in Southern History in April 2000 at Louisiana State University. Since 1937, this annual lecture series has had a widely recognized influence on the historical literature of the South; I am honored to have been invited to give the sixty-second series. What is no doubt less widely recognized—because one has to experience it in person—is the extraordinary graciousness that Louisiana State University and its History Department display in hosting these lectures. I would like especially to thank Paul Paskoff and Gaines M. Foster, who went well beyond the call of duty in making my wife and me feel at home during our stay in Baton Rouge, and William J. Cooper Jr., who helped arrange my visit but then had to miss my lectures, which coincided with his tenure as Douglas Southall Freeman Visiting Professor at the University of Richmond. They and their colleagues are experts in practicing true southern hospitality.

While preparing the Fleming Lectures, I was able to try out some of my ideas in a talk entitled "The American South in Comparative Perspective," given as the keynote address at the Commonwealth Fund Conference on the Two Souths: Toward an Agenda for Comparative Study of the American South and the Italian Mezzogiorno (University College London, January 1999). This address, along with many of the other conference papers, has been published in Enrico Dal Lago and Rick Halpern, eds., *The American South and the Italian Mezzogiorno: Essays in Comparative History* (Houndsmill, Eng.: Palgrave, 2002). I am grateful to Rick Halpern (then at

University College London, now at the University of Toronto) and Enrico Dal Lago (National University of Ireland, Galway) for hosting the conference and for inviting me to give this address; to Piero Bevilacqua for his incisive comments on it; and to Palgrave Macmillan for permission to republish portions of my keynote address in very different form.

Over the years, my graduate students at the University of Delaware have read and discussed portions of what eventually became this manuscript, and more generally have served as a sounding board for my ideas. I would particularly like to thank the members of my advanced seminar—Tracey Birdwell, Evelyn Causey, John Davies, Jeffrey Forret, Karen Ryder, and Christine Sears—for helping me to refine some of my arguments. At a later stage, two anonymous readers for Louisiana State University Press gave my book manuscript speedy, laudatory, and at the same time useful evaluations, thereby helping me improve the final product.

I am indebted to the many historians of the South—and to a smaller number of comparative historians—on whose efforts I have built. This is true not only because virtually all historians rely at least indirectly on the work of those who have preceded them, but also because, as an exercise in historiography as well as history, this volume pays a great deal of direct attention to that work. I have indicated many (although far from all) of these historians and their contributions in this volume's extensive footnotes, which are designed not only to document specific quotations and assertions but also to provide a kind of road map to some of the historical and historiographical controversies that lie at the heart of this study. I hope that those not mentioned will accept my collective acknowledgment of their scholarship, without which this book would have been impossible.

Although they have not read this book and are not responsible for any of its faults, a number of intellectual giants deserve mention here for having influenced my historical thinking at a general level. David Herbert Donald taught me to think analytically about the past, to question almost everything, and to strive for the kind of clarity of expression that indicates clarity of understanding; no one who was not a student of his can fully appreciate the impact of the training he provided. David M. Potter, C. Vann Woodward, David Brion Davis, and Eugene D. Genovese not only profoundly shaped (and in the latter two cases continue to shape) our understanding of the South and/or slavery but pioneered in insisting that this understanding requires a comparative framework; any exploration of the nineteenth-century South in comparative context must grapple with the many interpretive and methodological insights they produced. This book's title is derived from a remark of Potter's that "to writers for more than half a century the South has been a kind of sphinx on the American land"; see "The Enigma of the South" (1961), reprinted in his *The South and Sectional Conflict* (Baton Rouge: Louisiana State University Press, 1968), 4.

Then there is Howard N. Rabinowitz, who was my colleague during my nine years at the University of New Mexico (1976–85) and my friend until his untimely death at age fifty-six in 1998. A scholar of exceptionally broad interests, Rabinowitz was a historian of the South but also of cities, race relations, and ethnicity; although he did not call himself a comparative historian, he was one in the most basic sense of the term, because he always sought to understand the object of his attention within a more general context. Howard was a man of strong opinions, acerbic wit, passionate interests, and contempt for what he regarded as stupidity, hypocrisy, and faddishness. He would not have agreed with everything in this book, but I am sure that he would have recognized the extent to which he helped to shape it, not only through his innovative scholarship but also through the countless conversations we had on (among other things) history, politics, the South, and the state of the profession. This book's dedication speaks to my enormous regard for him as a scholar, colleague, and friend, and to the sense of loss engendered by his death.

Finally, I would like to thank my wife and colleague, Anne M. Boylan, who has been through every draft of this manuscript and who, as usual, has been my best—and favorite—critic.

INTRODUCTION

Historical study of the American South has exhibited a curiously dualistic character. On the one hand, there is its longstanding parochialism, its preoccupation with celebrating details of the past of interest mainly to southerners themselves; on the other, there is its cutting-edge creativity, its demonstration of how attention to a particular region can provide insights into subjects of scholarly interest far removed from regional antiquarianism. Long the province of southern whites—usually southern white men—southern history draws increasing attention from nonsoutherners and is increasingly central to the study of American history in general. Northern colleges routinely offer courses on the history of the South, and northern scholars are increasingly active in the field. Although the late Howard N. Rabinowitz, in an unfinished essay in which he described himself as the exceptional outsider in southern history, argued that "just about every American-born southern historian and certainly the major figures in the field, is either of or in the South,"[1] a very partial and arbitrary listing of some of the many nonsoutherners who have recently contributed to southern history reveals just how wrong the usually astute Rabinowitz was in this judgment: Kenneth M. Stampp, Leon F. Litwack, Jonathan M. Wiener, Kathleen M. Brown, Kenneth S. Greenberg, Christine Leigh Heyrman,

---

1. Noting that Harold D. Woodman and Carl N. Degler constituted exceptions to his generalization, Rabinowitz defined the South as "the former Confederacy plus Maryland and Delaware," a definition that I cannot help suspecting was designed at least in part to place *me* among the southerners; Howard N. Rabinowitz, "The Other as Southern Historian" (unpublished manuscript), 1.

Mark M. Smith, Drew Gilpin Faust, Steven Hahn, Stephanie Mc-
Curry, Michael Perman, Ira Berlin, Harold D. Woodman, Gavin
Wright, Catherine Clinton, Herbert G. Gutman, Eugene D. Genovese, William Dusinberre, William W. Freehling, Michael O'Brien,
Barbara J. Fields, Eric Foner, James Oakes, Peter Kolchin . . . Surely,
it should be clear that nonsoutherners now play a central role in
writing about the South, just as the South is increasingly central to
the study of American history in general. Bubba has arrived.[2]

Indeed, in many ways study of the South has become not just
Americanized but globalized. "Southern literature is a very big deal
among Japanese scholars," James C. Cobb noted recently in stressing the growing foreign fascination with the South, and "European
universities boast accomplished scholars whose principal interests
are the history, literature, and culture of the American South."[3] As
significant as this foreign interest in the South is a growing attention

2. In his 1986 presidential address, Carl N. Degler proclaimed himself the first president of the Southern Historical Association who was neither born nor currently working
in the South; Degler, "Thesis, Antithesis, Synthesis: The South, the North, and the Nation," *Journal of Southern History* 53 (February 1987): 3. Since then, of sixteen SHA presidents (including Degler), six were born outside the eleven former Confederate states and
six resided outside those states at the time of their presidency. The following is a chronological listing of the sixteen presidents, with their birth indicated by "S" or "N" and their
location by "s" or "n": Carl N. Degler (N, n), Willard B. Gatewood (S, s), Bennett H.
Wall (S, s), Louis R. Harlan (S, n), Don Higginbotham (N, s), August Meier (N, n),
Jimmie L. Franklin (S, n), Numan V. Bartley (S, s), Dan T. Carter (S, s), Harold D.
Woodman (N, n), Paul K. Conkin (S, s), Carol K. Bleser (S, s), James C. Cobb (S, s),
Drew Gilpin Faust (N, n), Bertram Wyatt-Brown (N, s). The preponderance of northern
scholars delivering the annual Walter Lynwood Fleming Lectures in Southern History
provides a more pronounced indication of the nationalization of southern history: of the
twenty Fleming lecturers between 1981 and 2000, only five were born in the South and
only eight held appointments (at the time of their lectureship) at colleges or universities
located in the South. In chronological order, they include: Jack P. Greene (N, n), Eric
Foner (N, n), Leon F. Litwack (N, n), Robert V. Remini (N, n), C. Vann Woodward
(S, n), Russell F. Weigley (N, n), Drew Gilpin Faust (N, n), Lewis P. Simpson (S, s),
Robert W. Johannsen (N, n), Harold D. Woodman (N, n), William E. Leuchtenburg
(N, s), Dan T. Carter (S, s), James M. McPherson (N, n), Jacqueline Dowd Hall (S, s),
Bertram Wyatt-Brown (N, s), James L. Axtell (S, s), Gavin Wright (N, n), Fred Colby
Hobson Jr. (S, s), Michael F. Holt (N, s), Peter Kolchin (N, n).

3. James C. Cobb, "Modernization and the Mind of the South," in his *Redefining
Southern Culture: Mind and Identity in the Modern South* (Athens: University of Georgia
Press, 1999), 209.

to developments abroad among students of the South, for if the South is central to American history, many of the most interesting topics in southern history—from slavery and the Civil War to questions of self-identity and relations among local, regional, and national authority—are by no means unique to the South and are therefore best understood in the context of similar developments elsewhere. It is hardly surprising, then, that as part of a broadened effort to come to grips with the South's past, revisionist work on the region exhibits a growing comparative dimension. Properly conceived, southern history can—and to some extent already does—lie at the forefront of efforts to make sense of human relations around the world. Bubba truly *has* arrived.

Needless to say, as both a southern and a comparative historian, I cannot but welcome this development. At the same time, I believe that it is important for us to think carefully about what we hope to learn from a widened focus, so as to control comparative history rather than let it control us. In this book, I would like to consider some of the benefits and problems of providing a comparative framework for southern history, looking both at how historians have approached the subject and at how we might best conceptualize the study of the South comparatively. Although historians have differed sharply in their definitions of "comparative history,"[4] here I use the concept loosely, to cover a variety of approaches and methodologies designed to accentuate context. In doing so, I hope simultaneously to explore and promote a particular kind of comparative history that I think is especially promising although it is rarely practiced: analysis that focuses on one case or locale but places it in a broader—

4. For some explorations of the nature and methodology of comparative history, see Raymond Grew, "The Case for Comparing Histories," *American Historical Review* 85 (October 1980): 763–82; George M. Fredrickson, "Comparative History," in *The Past Before Us: Contemporary Historical Writings in the United States,* ed. Michael Kammen (Ithaca, N.Y.: Cornell University Press, 1980), 457–73; A. A. Braembussche, "Historical Explanation and Comparative Method: Towards a Theory of the History of Society," *History and Theory* 28 (1989): 1–24; Peter Kolchin, "Comparing American History," *Reviews in American History* 10 (December 1982): 64–81; and Peter Kolchin, "The Comparative Approach to the Study of Slavery: Problems and Prospects" (unpublished paper delivered at conference on "Les Dépendances Serviles," Ecole des Hautes Etudes en Sciences Sociales, Paris, June 1996).

comparative—framework. Less *rigorously* comparative than "compare and contrast" studies that give equal weight to two cases or social-scientific works that produce theory and generalization by considering many cases, this "soft" approach can eliminate or reduce many of the problems of organization, focus, research, and expertise that have bedeviled and impeded the development of traditional comparison, while enabling the scholar to combine attention to two important historical components: specificity and context.

The chapters that follow set forth three different ways of considering the South in comparative context. In chapter 1, I consider comparisons between the South and the North, or what for comparative purposes one might call the "un-South." Because the very meaning of *South* is found in contrast to *North,* this is in some ways the most basic and obvious comparison, one that implicitly underlies virtually every generalization about the South; any statement about southern characteristics—"southerners are hospitable," "southerners are lazy"—draws its significance from the implied understanding that these characteristics in some way differentiate the South from the rest of the country. From efforts to define the South to generalizations about what happened in the South to considerations of how southerners and nonsoutherners conceived of the South, the context provided by the "un-South" provides the essential backdrop.

In chapter 2, I turn to a different kind of comparison, that among various components of what are in effect "many Souths." Although our understanding of *South* and *southerner* requires a contextual setting of un-South and unsoutherner, there has never been one South or one archetypal southerner: internal variations—whether geographic, class, religious, racial—complicate the picture and ultimately raise the question of whether one can properly speak of "the" South at all. The nearer one gets, the more pronounced and significant such variations become; a "southern" accent may be recognizable in Minnesota, but *within* the South few would confuse the speech heard in eastern Tennessee with that of southern Louisiana, lowcountry Georgia, or for that matter upcountry Georgia. If heterogeneity complicates the effort to generalize about the South and southerners, it also underlies a persisting struggle for control of southern identity. Including African Americans as southerners, to take one simple example, upends a lot of conventional judgments about "southern" characteristics.

In chapter 3, I undertake still a third kind of comparative analysis, examining the South in the context of societies outside the United States that have shared some of the same attributes and can therefore be termed "other Souths." Because some of the most important questions in southern history—from slavery to regional identity— are also central to the history of other societies, an examination of those questions and their relationship to southern history can benefit from a broadened geographic framework. Although this kind of comparison is useful for what it tells us about both general developments and those in the South, my primary concern in these pages is on the latter; the focus remains on the South, albeit in comparative context. After exploring a variety of ways in which the South can be considered in a broad international setting, I pay particular attention to the comparison between the emancipation of the southern slaves and the Russian serfs—a subject that has engaged my research for some time—and on what this comparison can offer to southern historians. As with the "un-South," so too with "other Souths" considering southern developments in light of those elsewhere can provide new insights by placing them in a new perspective.

My treatment of these subjects is both selective and wide-ranging: although my focus is on the nineteenth-century South, which encompasses a set of topics—slavery, emancipation, the Civil War— that lend themselves particularly well to comparative elucidation of important questions such as regional distinctiveness and the extent of continuity versus change, I do not hesitate to draw observations from both the colonial era and the twentieth century when those observations seem appropriate. Topically, too, my approach is selective and wide-ranging. Unlike contemporary observers, historians have typically been more comfortable comparing specific features of southern society—whether economic growth, social structure, or food—than making broad societal comparisons between the South and North or the South and other "souths," and in its historiographical guise this book of necessity follows suit. Nevertheless, I also deal with both popular and scholarly efforts to define and characterize the South as a whole, efforts that are at least implicitly comparative.

Throughout this volume, I have paid particular attention to the Civil War, emancipation, and southern identity, no doubt in part because these themes interest me but more importantly because they are so central to southern history. They are, of course, closely interrelated: if southern emancipation was atypical in its wartime origin, it was the freeing of the slaves that more than anything else lent significance to the Civil War and rendered it a revolutionary upheaval rather than simply a bloody conflagration. Similarly, the process of emancipation reveals more graphically than any other single event the contested nature of southern identity, the extent to which the meaning of "South" and "southern" were—and still are—up for grabs. A comparative perspective, I believe, casts these hotly debated subjects in new light.

In short, this book is at once speculative and substantive, an exercise in regional history and in historical comparison, a work of history and of historiography. Perhaps more than anything, it should be regarded as an extended analytical essay designed to explore old questions in new ways.

I THE SOUTH AND THE UN-SOUTH

Persistent observations of basic differences between the North and South date from the last third of the eighteenth century, when substantial numbers of northerners and southerners were first thrust together. Spending a year in 1773–74 as a plantation tutor on the Virginia estate of Robert Carter III, Philip Vickers Fithian was amazed by the differences he found between his temporary residence and his native New Jersey, differences that were manifested in everything from religion, economy, social structure, and manners to food, race relations, family life, and use of leisure time. Noting that he would find the Virginians' "manner of living . . . in many respects different from any thing you have been accustomed to," Fithian predicted to his successor in tutoring—also a northerner—that "you will be making ten thousand Comparisons." Although some of the contrasts that Fithian delineated clearly reflected the class and religious gap between his controlled, middle-class, Presbyterian home and the relaxed, aristocratic, Anglican world he found at Nomini Hall, Fithian's remarkable *Journal and Letters* presents a compelling case for an early cultural deviation—and for recognition of this deviation—between South and North, even as prominent residents of both sections groped toward making common cause against what they defined as British "tyranny."[1]

1. *Journal & Letters of Philip Vickers Fithian, 1773–1774: A Plantation Tutor of the Old Dominion,* ed. Hunter Dickinson Farish (Charlottesville: University Press of Virginia, 1957), 167. For development of the argument that a self-conscious South first emerged during the American Revolution, see John Alden, *The First South* (Baton Rouge: Louisiana State University Press, 1961).

A decade later, Thomas Jefferson raised North-South distinctions to a more generalized level in his famous letter to a French aristocrat, the Marquis de Chastellux. Positing a sharp geographic gradation, Jefferson suggested that "an observant traveler, without the aid of the quadrant may always know his latitude by the character of the people among whom he finds himself." Listing in separate columns the contrasting traits of northerners and southerners, he proclaimed that "in the North they are cool, sober, laborious, persevering, independent, jealous of their own liberties, and just to those of others, interested, chicaning, superstitious and hypocritical in their religion"; by contrast, "in the South they are fiery, Voluptuary, indolent, unsteady, independent, zealous for their own liberties, but trampling on those of others, generous, candid, without attachment or pretensions to any religion but that of the heart." With the exception of his observations on religion, which were soon rendered obsolete by the evangelical revivals that reshaped the South's religious landscape, Jefferson's characterizations entered the conventional wisdom as antebellum Americans adopted the familiar stereotypes of the southern "Cavalier" and the northern "Yankee."[2]

Even as these traditional stereotypes persisted, they continued to evolve. During the late antebellum period, belief in a particular variant of southern distinctiveness that emphasized the South's backwardness gained increasing ascendancy in much of the United States. The image of a backward South was already latent if underdeveloped in the writings of Fithian and Jefferson, but it assumed far greater salience as the struggle over the expansion of slavery came

2. Jefferson to Chastellux, 2 September 1785, *The Portable Thomas Jefferson*, ed. Merrill D. Peterson (New York: Viking Press, 1975), 388, 387. On the evangelical transformation of southern Protestantism, see John B. Boles, *The Great Revival, 1787–1805: The Origins of the Southern Evangelical Mind* (Lexington: University Press of Kentucky, 1972); and Christine Leigh Heyrman, *Southern Cross: The Beginnings of the Bible Belt* (New York: Alfred A. Knopf, 1997). On the antebellum evolution of southern stereotypes, see William R. Taylor, *Cavalier and Yankee: The Old South and American National Character* (New York: George Braziller, 1961); and Susan-Mary Grant, *North Over South: Northern Nationalism and American Identity in the Antebellum Era* (Lawrence: University Press of Kansas, 2000).

to dominate American politics and the gulf between North and South seemed to widen. To northern observers such as Frederick Law Olmsted, who reported in the *New York Times* on a series of travels through the South in the 1850s, southerners appeared poor, slovenly, ignorant, and degraded—practically a foreign people who enjoyed virtually none of the normal amenities of civilized life. Noting that he sought whenever possible to stay in the houses of well-to-do people "recommended to me by disinterested persons on the road as being better than ordinary," Olmsted reported that in these houses he "found no garden, no flowers, no fruit, no tea, no cream, no sugar, no bread . . . no curtains, no lifting windows (three times out of four absolutely no windows), no couch—if one reclined in the family room it was on the bare floor—for there were no carpets or mats. . . . From the banks of the Mississippi to the banks of James," he complained, "I did not (that I remember) see, except perhaps in one or two towns, a thermometer, nor a book of Shakespeare, nor a piano-forte or sheet of music . . . or a work of art of the slightest merit." Even the much-vaunted southern hospitality proved elusive: Olmsted noted that "only twice, in a journey of four thousand miles, . . . did I receive a night's lodging or a repast from a native Southerner, without having the exact price in money which I was expected to pay for it stated to me by those at whose hands I received it."[3]

Despite the multiple assertions of "new" Souths and "disappear-

3. Frederick Law Olmsted, *The Cotton Kingdom: A Traveller's Observations on Cotton and Slavery in the American Slave States* (1861), ed. Arthur M. Schlesinger Sr., intro. Lawrence N. Powell (New York: Random House, 1984), 520, 550. On antebellum northern images of the backward South, see Eric Foner, *Free Soil, Free Labor, Free Men: The Ideology of the Republican Party Before the Civil War* (New York: Oxford University Press, 1970); and Grant, *North Over South*. The notion of a backward South was by no means exclusively northern: although they did not always subscribe to all the negative elements of southern character found in Olmsted's writings, a wide range of antebellum southerners—from critics of the social order such as Hinton Helper to defenders of it such as J. D. B. De Bow—accepted some version of southern backwardness. See Hinton Rowan Helper, *The Impending Crisis of the South: How to Meet It* (New York: Burdick Brothers, 1857); and J. D. B. De Bow, *The Industrial Resources of the Southern and Western States* (New Orleans: De Bow's Review, 1852), e.g., II, 113–14.

ing" Souths to which we have become accustomed during the past century and a half,[4] these traditional stereotypes have proved remarkably enduring, captured in summary by John F. Kennedy's supposed quip that Washington, D.C., was a city characterized by northern charm and southern efficiency. The theme of southern backwardness persisted in numerous variations, reflected in literary depictions, in the discovery and rediscovery of southern poverty whether among Alabama sharecroppers in the 1930s or Appalachian miners in the 1950s, in the struggle to overcome the South's Jim Crow regime, and in caricatures of southern rednecks in popular television programs such as *Hee Haw, The Dukes of Hazard,* and *Beverly Hillbillies.* Although with slight modification southern backwardness could be turned into a positive attribute and embraced as an antidote to (variously) American capitalism, materialism, liberalism, radicalism, secularism, or modernism run rampant, it was more often associated with a starkly negative view that accentuated south-

---

4. Noting that "for as long as people have believed there was a South they have also believed that it was disappearing," Edward L. Ayers observed that the section, although "perpetually fading, seems to be perpetually with us"; see Ayers, "What We Talk About When We Talk About the South," in Ayers et al., *All Over the Map: Rethinking American Regions* (Baltimore: Johns Hopkins University Press, 1996), 68, 69. On the continuing southern obsession with distinctiveness even as that distinctiveness declined and America itself became increasingly southernized, see James C. Cobb, "Modernization and the Mind of the South," in his *Redefining Southern Culture: Mind and Identity in the Modern South* (Athens: University of Georgia Press, 1999), esp. 206–208. Howard N. Rabinowitz identified at least four major "New Souths" between the 1870s and the 1970s; see his *The First New South: 1865–1920* (Arlington Heights, Ill.: Harlan Davidson, 1992), 1. "Nearly every decade since the late-nineteenth century has heralded a nascent New South," wrote Joe P. Dunn in his preface to *The Future South: A Historical Perspective for the Twenty-First Century,* ed. Joe P. Dunn and Howard L. Preston (Urbana: University of Illinois Press, 1991), 1. For one of many lamentations over the decline of southern distinctiveness, see John Egerton, *The Americanization of Dixie: The Southernization of America* (New York: Harper's Magazine Press, 1974). For the contrary view, that even as it increasingly influences American culture, the South "is still fighting most of its oldest battles," see Peter Applebome, *Dixie Rising: How the South Is Shaping American Values, Politics, and Culture* (New York: Random House, 1996), 14. For the continuing scholarly debate, see Robert P. Steed, Lawrence W. Moreland, and Tod A. Baker, eds., *The Disappearing South: Studies in Regional Change and Continuity* (Tuscaloosa: University of Alabama Press, 1990).

ern deficiencies. Such negative images of the South reached their peak during the 1950s and 1960s, when, to a generation inspired by the struggle for civil rights, the South appeared as hopelessly retrograde as it had to antebellum opponents of slavery. Describing (and endorsing as accurate) the "Southern Mystique," which he qualified as the "American mystique about the South," historian Howard Zinn captured most of the salient elements of this stereotype, characterizing the region as not only racist but also "provincial, conservative, fundamentalist, nativist, violent, conformist, militaristic."[5]

In the post–civil rights era, a softer perception of the South—one owing more to Jefferson than to Olmsted—seems to have edged out the most negative images of the backward South in popular American consciousness. In my undergraduate course on the Old South, I spend part of the first meeting discussing with the students the question of southern distinctiveness, in both the past and the present; invariably, the great majority of these students—including those from the South—ignore variations among southerners and emphasize a set of well-worn cultural stereotypes most of which would have been familiar to Jefferson: southerners, they tell me, are slow, laid-back, courteous, friendly, generous, hot-headed, honorable, hospitable, and locally oriented. (These judgments are similar to those elicited by Edward L. Ayers in a poll at the University of Virginia, where students "commented most on the South's cour-

---

5. Howard Zinn, *The Southern Mystique* (New York: Alfred A. Knopf, 1964), 217. For varied depictions of southern poverty and backwardness, see Erskine Caldwell, *Tobacco Road* (New York: C. Scribner's Sons, 1932); James Agee and Walker Evans, *Let Us Now Praise Famous Men* (Boston: Houghton Mifflin, 1941); Michael Harrington, *The Other America: Poverty in the United States* (New York: Macmillan, 1962). On changing popular perceptions of the South, see Jack Temple Kirby, *Media-Made Dixie: The South in the American Imagination* (Baton Rouge: Louisiana State University Press, 1978). For the most famous positive reconfiguration of southern backwardness, see the collection by "Twelve Southerners," *I'll Take My Stand: The South and the Agrarian Tradition* (New York: Harper & Brothers, 1930). See Michael O'Brien, *The Idea of the American South, 1920–1941* (Baltimore: Johns Hopkins University Press, 1979); and Paul K. Conkin, *The Southern Agrarians* (Knoxville: University of Tennessee Press, 1988). Unlike most other observers, Zinn, in noting that the Southern Mystique "is beginning to vanish," *welcomed* the decline of southern distinctiveness (3).

tesy, hospitality, sense of history, and natural beauty.") In making such pronouncements, they seem remarkably unfamiliar with the South of Zinn's "Southern Mystique."[6]

Nevertheless, despite their differences, the two versions of the South (and others in between) share at least three essential characteristics. First, many of their most noteworthy components differ more in normative than in substantive terms (and are therefore less at odds than they first appear): both, for example, see the South as characterized by a slower pace of life, but whereas one celebrates this trait as a hallmark of sanity in a world hurtling out of control the other condemns it as evidence of backwardness and inefficiency. Equally important, the two versions share the assumption that the South and southerners differ fundamentally from the North and northerners, and the implicit understanding that coming to grips with the South's character makes sense only in a broader, American context.

The debate among historians has taken a somewhat different turn. Although some have addressed the question of southern versus northern character,[7] most have been leery of assigning a universal, homogenized personality to either northerners or southerners, preferring to explore sectional distinctiveness in terms of the social, economic, and political order. It is also worth noting that, whether consciously or unconsciously, historians have typically followed other Americans in using the term *southern* to apply primarily to *white* southerners, in the process—as I shall argue in chapter 2— playing down an important element of diversity that in fact has characterized the South. Whatever the focus, however, the effort to come to grips with the nature of the South has meaning only in terms of distinguishing the section from what it was not—the *un*-South.

6. Ayers, "What We Talk About When We Talk About the South," 124. Polling over three hundred undergraduate students, white and black, northern and southern, Ayers found that only when it came to the question of racism did white and black perceptions of southern characteristics diverge: "African-Americans ranked racism fourth [among leading southern characteristics], whereas white students ranked it tenth" (124).

7. See, for example, David Bertelson, *The Lazy South* (New York: Oxford University Press, 1967); and John Hope Franklin, *The Militant South, 1800–1861* (Cambridge, Mass.: Harvard University Press, 1956).

Scholars have differed sharply over what set the South off from the North, and have enunciated a long list of items—some frivolous and others significant, some overlapping and others contradictory—that supposedly made the South southern. If to some the South is marked by people who eat grits, speak with a "drawl," and tell stories, others have emphasized as a "central theme" of southern history white supremacy, a hot and humid climate, Celtic heritage, or a culture of honor.[8] Many scholars have seen violence—from duels and backcountry brawls among people of equal status to savage repression of subordinates who stepped out of bounds—as an essential southern characteristic.[9] Often, an *implicit* understanding of what

8. Ulrich B. Phillips, "The Central Theme of Southern History," *American Historical Review* 34 (1928): 30–43; A. Cash Koeniger, "Climate and Southern Distinctiveness," *Journal of Southern History* 54 (February 1988): 21–44; Grady McWhiney, *Cracker Culture: Celtic Ways in the Old South* (University, Ala.: University of Alabama Press, 1988); Bertram Wyatt-Brown, *Southern Honor: Ethics and Behavior in the Old South* (New York: Oxford University Press, 1982), and *The Shaping of Southern Culture: Honor, Grace, and War, 1760s–1880s* (Chapel Hill: University of North Carolina Press, 2001); Kenneth S. Greenberg, *Honor & Slavery* (Princeton: Princeton University Press, 1996). See David L. Smiley, "The Quest for the Central Theme in Southern History," *South Atlantic Quarterly* 71 (Summer 1972): 307–25.

9. Franklin, *The Militant South*; Edward L. Ayers, *Vengeance and Justice: Crime and Punishment in the 19th-Century South* (New York: Oxford University Press, 1984), esp. 3–33; Eliott J. Gorn, " 'Gouge and Bite, Pull Hair and Scratch': The Social Significance of Fighting in the Backcountry," *American Historical Review* 90 (February 1985): 18–43; Roger Lane, *Murder in America: A History* (Columbus: Ohio State University Press, 1997), 149–50, 350–51, and passim. For the argument that mob violence in the antebellum South was both qualitatively and quantitatively different from that in the North, see David Grimsted, *American Mobbing, 1828–1861: Toward Civil War* (New York: Oxford University Press, 1998). For two important books on political violence in the postbellum South, see George C. Rable, *But There Was No Peace: The Role of Violence in the Politics of Reconstruction* (Athens: University of Georgia Press, 1984); and Kenneth C. Barnes, *Who Killed John Clayton? Political Violence and the Emergence of the New South, 1861–1893* (Durham: Duke University Press, 1998). On lynching, see Stewart E. Tolnay and E. M. Beck, *A Festival of Violence: An Analysis of Southern Lynching, 1882–1930* (Urbana: University of Illinois Press, 1995); and W. Fitzhugh Brundage, *Lynching in the New South: Georgia and Virginia, 1880–1930* (Urbana: University of Illinois Press, 1993). A continuing form of violence against subordinates is evident in the widespread acceptance throughout much of the South of corporal punishment (both private and institutional) of children. In 1997–98, "ten states accounted for more than 90 percent of the reported incidents" of school paddling nationwide; of these, only New Mexico was neither a southern nor bor-

southern means is evident in the titles or key phrases of scholarly works, as when Christopher Morris refers to Warren County, Mississippi, "becoming southern" between 1770 and 1860, or James C. Cobb dubs the Mississippi Delta "the most southern place on earth," or Christine Heyrman argues that Protestant evangelicals scored major gains in the early-nineteenth-century South only when they "learned to speak with a southern accent."[10]

Although these attempts to make sense of southern "southernness" have contributed greatly to our understanding of the South, they have typically been stronger as efforts to *describe* than to *explain* or *define* the South. Virtually none of the most important characteristics usually emphasized as southern is *exclusively* southern: the nineteenth-century South was hardly alone, for example, in being overwhelmingly rural and agricultural, exhibiting high levels of racism and violence, or displaying a variety of "premodern" values. (Adopting an agricultural economy or rural population as defining southern traits requires one to conclude that Minnesota was more southern in 1850 than Georgia, a judgment that is obviously problematical.) Indeed, in a clever but ultimately unsatisfactory effort to overcome the problem that such shared characteristics pose for defining the South, Howard Zinn suggested that what made the South southern was precisely its extreme Americanness. If southerners were unusually violent in a *national* context, Americans themselves were unusually violent in a broader *international* context, and southern violence was in fact quintessentially American; the unattractive traits that made up Zinn's Southern Mystique were really unattractive *American* traits, for the South "crystallizes the defects of"—indeed "is really the *essence* of"—the United States as a whole.[11] More notable as moral judgment than as analytical device,

der state. "Lawsuits Touch Off Debate Over Paddling in the Schools," *New York Times,* 3 May 2001, A1, A20 (quotation: A20).

10. Christopher Morris, *Becoming Southern: The Evolution of a Way of Life, Warren County and Vicksburg, Mississippi, 1770–1860* (New York: Oxford University Press, 1995); James C. Cobb, *The Most Southern Place on Earth: The Mississippi Delta and the Roots of Regional Identity* (New York: Oxford University Press, 1992); Heyrman, *Southern Cross,* 27.

11. Zinn, *The Southern Mystique,* 217–62 (quotation: 218).

Zinn's ingenious thesis allowed him to bash southern values without sanctimoniously seeming to put forth superior American values, but it did not help very much in understanding the *peculiar* nature of the South. In making sense of the controversy over southern distinctiveness, the key question must be a comparative one: what important experiences have most southerners shared with each other that most northerners have *not* shared (or at least that most northerners have shared in doses small enough to constitute qualitatively different experiences)?

When the question is phrased in this manner, I think it is clear that the two characteristics that were most instrumental in setting the South off from the rest of the country—in shaping if not defining a nineteenth-century South—are slavery and the Confederate rebellion. Each of these alone became a prime signifier of "southernness." Antebellum Americans identified the South so closely with slavery that they typically linked the two words together—the "slave South"—and perceived someone who was antislavery to be antisouthern. Slavery's continued existence in border states that seemed only partially southern reinforces the utility of using the Peculiar Institution to measure southernness, since their borderline character as southern corresponds to their borderline character as slaveowning: Maryland, whose population in 1860 was 12.7 percent slave, did not appear nearly so southern as Mississippi, with 55.2 percent slaves, and Delaware, where only 1.6 percent of residents were slaves and 91.7 percent of blacks were free, hardly seemed southern at all.[12]

Equally powerful in distinguishing South from North was the Civil War. Indeed, in popular parlance the war pitted the North against the South and the defeat of the Confederacy marked the triumph of the former over the latter. But not only can slave density and support for the Confederacy each be used as an index of "southernness"; the two criteria provide virtually the same measure of

12. Using slavery as an implicit criterion for southernness, William W. Freehling noted that "at Delaware, the coastal South's northeastern edge, southernness almost evaporated"; Freehling, *The Road to Disunion: Secessionists at Bay, 1776–1854* (New York: Oxford University Press, 1990), 32. Statistics in this and the following paragraph are from Peter Kolchin, *American Slavery, 1619–1877* (New York: Hill & Wang, 1993), 242.

southernness. If the thirty-three United States are divided into four categories of "southernness" based on the level of their support for the Confederate rebellion, exactly the same categories emerge from a ranking of those states by degree of slaveholding: slaves averaged 46.0 percent of the population in the seven Deep South states that seceded before the firing on Fort Sumter, 28.6 percent in the four Upper South states that seceded after Fort Sumter, 10.9 percent in the four border slave-states that remained in the Union, and 0 percent in the remaining eighteen northern states. The distribution of southern states in the first three categories was as follows:

EARLY SECEDERS (average=46.0 percent slaves)

South Carolina	57.2	Florida	44.0
Mississippi	55.2	Georgia	43.7
Louisiana	46.9	Texas	30.2
Alabama	45.1		

LATE SECEDERS (average=28.6 percent slaves)

North Carolina	33.4	Arkansas	25.5
Virginia	30.7	Tennessee	24.8

LOYAL STATES (average=10.9 percent slaves)

Kentucky	19.5	Missouri	9.7
Maryland	12.7	Delaware	1.6

The convergence between slavery and support for secession as indices of southernness indicates, of course, the extent to which the Confederacy represented a proslavery rebellion, a truth now widely accepted by historians and receiving its most recent confirmation in Charles B. Dew's analysis of the speeches and writings of the "Secession Commissioners" sent by five Deep South states to promote secession throughout the South.[13] It also suggests that in some ways

13. Charles B. Dew, *Apostles of Disunion: Southern Secession Commissioners and the Causes of the Civil War* (Charlottesville: University Press of Virginia, 2001). For additional evidence that both slaveowners and Confederate leaders saw the war as one for slavery, see James L. Roark, *Masters Without Slaves: Southern Planters in the Civil War*

the most salient southern experience—one at the intersection of slavery and Civil War—was emancipation, a subject to which I shall devote considerable attention throughout this volume.

Although slavery and the Civil War work particularly well in defining the *nineteenth-*century South, these criteria are also pertinent for earlier and later eras. True, in colonial America slavery existed in all of the colonies, but only in the South did it reach a level at which one can speak of a true "slave society" rather than a society with some slaves, a distinction that has received careful elaboration in Ira Berlin's recent book, *Many Thousands Gone.* Although neither slavery nor the Confederacy survived 1865, grappling with their *legacy* remains central to most efforts to give meaning to the modern southern experience. As C. Vann Woodward pointed out, the South differs from the rest of the United States in having endured military defeat, and the Civil War remains a vital component in the collective memory of southerners in a way that it does not for most northerners; only in the South can it still be assumed that "the war" means the Civil War rather than some more recent engagement such as World War II or Vietnam. Indeed, David Goldfield has recently argued that only after 1865, through their continuing verbal refighting of the war, did (white) southerners create a "distinct South." As central to modern southern history as confronting *the* war has been overcoming the legacy of slavery, from the Reconstruction effort to make citizens of former slaves to the attempt in the so-called "second Reconstruction" almost a century later to complete the work done by abolition. Just as slavery and the Confederacy are mutually reinforcing in defining the nineteenth-century South, so too are their legacies closely intertwined as southerners grapple with what it means to be southern in the modern era—a point clearly symbolized by the attachment of segregationists to the Confederate flag as the

---

and Reconstruction (New York: W. W. Norton, 1977), 1–32, 68–108; and Drew Gilpin Faust, *The Creation of Confederate Nationalism: Ideology and Identity in the Civil War South* (Baton Rouge: Louisiana State University Press, 1988), 59–60. For the argument that it was their commitment to slavery that "made Southerners believe that they constituted a separate nation," see John McCardell, *The Idea of a Southern Nation: Southern Nationalists and Southern Nationalism, 1830–1860* (New York: W. W. Norton, 1979), 4.

descendants of slaves sought to go to school with the descendants of slaveowners.[14]

Because the Civil War constituted a war for southern independence, it has inevitably stood at the center of scholarly efforts to explore the question of southern distinctiveness—what it meant to be southern. Historians have disagreed sharply over the extent to which the war was a product of fundamental differences between North and South. During the late nineteenth and early twentieth centuries, most historians believed that it was. Some stressed the gap between Yankee and Cavalier cultures; others accentuated the moral conflict between defenders and opponents of slavery; still others saw an irreconcilable political struggle between those committed to states' rights and those who sought to impose a unified national state. The most influential explanation, however, consisted of the economic argument—which received its most famous enunciation in Charles and Mary Beard's classic *Rise of American Civilization*—that the Civil War constituted a "Second American Revolution" (in fact, America's first *real* revolution) in which northern masters of capital seized control of the country from the slave-based plantation aristocracy that dominated the agrarian South. Drawing a direct analogy with the French Revolution, the Beards argued that the conflicting political interests of planters and industrial capitalists reflected increasingly sharp socioeconomic differences between the two sections, differences that could only be resolved by the "social cataclysm in which the capitalists, laborers, and farmers of the North drove from power in the national government the planting aristocracy of the South."[15]

14. Ira Berlin, *Many Thousands Gone: The First Two Centuries of Slavery in North America* (Cambridge, Mass.: Harvard University Press, 1998); C. Vann Woodward, "The Irony of Southern History" (1953), in Woodward, *The Burden of Southern History* (New York: Vintage Books, 1961), 167–91; David Goldfield, *Still Fighting the Civil War: The American South and Southern History* (Baton Rouge: Louisiana State University Press, 2002), 2.

15. Charles A. Beard and Mary R. Beard, *The Rise of American Civilization*, 2 vols. (New York: Macmillan, 1928), II, ch. 18 (quotation: 54). For a thorough treatment of early "difference" interpretations, see Thomas J. Pressly, *Americans Interpret Their Civil War* (1954; New York: Collier Books, 1962), 149–262.

Beginning in the 1920s and drawing increasing support in the "consensus" years after World War II, "revisionist" historians played down differences between North and South. Suggesting that the Civil War was a "needless war" brought on by a "blundering generation," scholars such as Charles W. Ramsdell, Avery O. Craven, James G. Randall, and Frank L. Owsley insisted that slavery was a false issue: few northerners shared the abolitionists' concern for the plight of the southern bondsmen, most southern whites were yeoman farmers, and in any case the Peculiar Institution had reached its "natural limits" and soon would have declined on its own. Although a small band of black and Marxist scholars resisted the new orthodoxy, most historians at midcentury agreed that had it not been for extremist agitators, southerners and northerners would have been able to work out whatever minor differences they had. The new mood was caught well by publication in 1960 of a volume entitled *The Southerner as American,* in which nine prominent historians rejected what they regarded as exaggerated claims for southern distinctiveness. "The traditional emphasis on the South's differentness and on the conflict between Southernism and Americanism is wrong historically," explained the volume's editor. "We all agree that the most important fact about the Southerner is that he has been throughout his history also an American."[16]

Since the 1960s, a growing number of historians have reasserted

16. Charles Grier Sellers Jr., ed., *The Southerner as American* (Chapel Hill: University of North Carolina Press, 1960), vi–vii. The gender assumption inherent in this version of southernness is also noteworthy; see chapter 2, below, for a discussion of how attention to women has reshaped our understandings of the South. As late as 1979, historian Michael O'Brien cited the Sellers volume in referring to a "partial consensus" on the South's essential Americanness; see his *Idea of the American South,* xii. For examples of Civil War "revisionism," see Charles W. Ramsdell, "The Natural Limits of Slavery Expansion," *Mississippi Valley Historical Review* 16 (September 1929): 151–71; Avery O. Craven, *The Repressible Conflict, 1830–1861* (Baton Rouge: Louisiana State University Press, 1939); and James G. Randall, "The Blundering Generation," *Mississippi Valley Historical Review* 27 (June 1940): 3–28. For examples of dissenting interpretations by black and Marxist scholars, see W. E. B. Du Bois, *Black Reconstruction in America, 1860–1880* (1935; New York: Atheneum, 1973), esp. 3–83; and James S. Allen, *Reconstruciton: The Battle for Democracy (1856–1876)* (New York: International Publishers, 1937), esp. 17–28. See Pressly, *Americans Interpret Their Civil War,* esp. 289–328.

the importance of differences between North and South, even as others have continued to minimize those differences. As emphasis on diversity, conflict, and discontinuity replaced the search for common elements shared by all Americans, it once again became fashionable to see the Civil War as the product of a revolutionary conflict between the slave South and the free-labor North; as Eric Foner noted, "the term 'revolution' has reappeared in the most recent literature as a way of describing the Civil War and Reconstruction."[17] At the same time, however, a significant number of historians continued to deny that basic differences between North and South produced the war. Just as some scholars rediscovered and updated Beard's idea of a Second American Revolution, others developed a more sophisticated version of the blundering-generation thesis. Michael F. Holt and William E. Gienapp, for example, argued that the war resulted less from basic differences between northerners and southerners than from their shared commitment to "liberty" and "republicanism."[18]

Two prominent essays illustrate the continuing debate over this question. Asking "How Different from Each Other Were the Antebellum North and South," historian Edward Pessen came down squarely on the side of similarity. Maintaining that "Southern plant-

17. Eric Foner, *Reconstruction, 1863–1877: America's Unfinished Revolution* (New York: Harper & Row, 1988), xxiv. For an interesting new analysis that explains secession as "the result of imperatives in southern male culture—shaped by slavery"—operating within a distinctive "noninstitutional political culture," see Christopher J. Olsen, *Political Culture and Secession in Mississippi: Masculinity, Honor, and the Antiparty Tradition, 1830–1860* (New York: Oxford University Press, 2000), quotations: 195, 5. For a CD-ROM archive enabling students to delve into secession-era similarities and differences between two Shenandoah Valley communities—one northern (Franklin County, Pennsylvania) and the other southern (Augusta County, Virginia)—see Edward L. Ayers and Anne S. Rubin, eds., *Valley of the Shadow: Two Communities in the American Civil War: The Eve of War* (New York: W. W. Norton, 2000).

18. Michael F. Holt, *The Political Crisis of the 1850s* (New York: John Wiley & Sons, 1978), and *The Rise and Fall of the American Whig Party: Jacksonian Politics and the Onset of the Civil War* (New York: Oxford University Press, 1999); William E. Gienapp, *The Origins of the Republican Party, 1852–1856* (New York: Oxford University Press, 1987). An earlier version of this thesis is evident in David Donald, "An Excess of Democracy: The American Civil War and the Social Process," in his *Lincoln Reconsidered: Essays on the Civil War Era*, 2ᵈ ed. (New York: Vintage Books, 1961), 209–36.

ers had the attitudes and goals . . . of capitalistic businessmen," he argued that "the South's political system . . . like its hierarchical social structure, conformed closely to the prevailing arrangements in the North." Concluding that "the antebellum North and South were far more alike than the conventional scholarly wisdom has led us to believe," Pessen suggested that their coming to blows "may have been due, as is often the case when great powers fight, as much to their similarities as to their differences." But writing three years later, James M. McPherson reached a diametrically opposite conclusion. "Antebellum Americans certainly thought that North and South had evolved separate societies," he noted, "with institutions, interests, values, and ideologies so incompatible, so much in deadly conflict that they could no longer live together in the same nation." Pointing to contrasts in "urbanization, industrialization, labor force, demographic structure, violence and martial values, education, and attitudes toward change," he suggested that contemporary perceptions of difference were largely accurate.[19]

At the heart of this controversy is the question of to what extent slavery set the antebellum South off from the rest of the country. Here, too, longstanding disagreements remain unbridged. To oversimplify a complex and highly charged debate, one can divide historians of the slave South into two broad categories. On the one side are those such as Stanley L. Engerman, Robert W. Fogel, and James Oakes, who stress the profit-orientation of slaveholders and portray southern slavery as preeminently capitalistic. On the other is a group of historians represented most prominently by Eugene D. Genovese, who note the nonmarket relationship between master and slave and see southern slavery as a noncapitalist social formation that produced an increasingly distinctive economy, social order, and set of values.[20]

19. Edward Pessen, "How Different from Each Other Were the Antebellum North and South?" *American Historical Review* 85 (December 1980): 1146, 1147, 1148; James M. McPherson, "Antebellum Southern Exceptionalism: A New Look at an Old Question" (1983), reprinted in McPherson, *Drawn with the Sword: Reflections on the American Civil War* (New York: Oxford University Press, 1996), 3–23 (quotations: 7, 20).

20. Examples of the first group include Robert William Fogel and Stanley L. Engerman, *Time on the Cross: The Economics of American Negro Slavery*, 2 vols. (New York: Little, Brown, 1974); Robert William Fogel, *Without Consent or Contract: The Rise and Fall of American Slavery*, with 4 supplementary volumes (New York: Norton, 1989); and

Partially grounded in different understandings of capitalism, this debate is of more than semantic significance because it has important interpretive implications. Those who stress slavery's capitalist nature typically base their argument on the masters' commercial orientation. In their formulation, slavery emerges as simply another business—in Fogel's words, "a flexible, highly developed form of capitalism"—and southern slaveowners emerge as particular variants of businessmen, not all that different from their northern cousins; as Oakes put it, in "fundamental ways, the slaveholding experience coincided with the American experience at large." Those on the other side point to the nonmarket nature of southern *productive* relations, which differed fundamentally from the "free-labor" relationship between employer and employee; these scholars almost invariably move on to explore how this distinctive slave relationship brought with it a distinctive social order. It is worth noting that in doing so, they approach the question in much the same way that antebellum Americans did: rather than seeing the essence of capitalism as entrepreneurialism and stressing what southern planters and northern businessmen had in common, antebellum observers typically focused on the status of *labor,* distinguishing between the free-labor North and the slave-labor South. In short, categorizing the social order from the top down, in terms of opportunities for capital, is likely to yield a portrait of the South that accentuates its similarities with the North, whereas approaching the social order from the bottom up, with emphasis on the condition of labor, leads almost inevitably to a contrary portrait that asserts the South's distinctiveness. Clearly, definitions matter, and the comparative historian needs to pay careful attention to how words are used.[21]

James Oakes, *The Ruling Race: A History of American Slaveholders* (New York: Knopf, 1982). Examples of the second include Eugene D. Genovese, *The Political Economy of Slavery: Studies in the Economy and Society of the Slave South* (New York: Pantheon, 1965), and *Roll, Jordan, Roll: The World the Slaves Made* (New York: Pantheon, 1974); Elizabeth Fox-Genovese, *Within the Plantation Household: Black and White Women of the Old South* (Chapel Hill: University of North Carolina Press, 1988); and Kolchin, *American Slavery.*

21. See Douglas R. Egerton, "Markets Without a Market Revolution: Southern Planters and Capitalism," *Journal of the Early Republic* 16 (Summer 1996): 207–21. Quotations are from Fogel, *Without Consent or Contract,* 64; and Oakes, *The Ruling Race,* 227. On antebellum enunciation of the central distinction between slave labor and free

Aside from definitions, two other considerations deserve attention as historians seek to make sense of conflicting claims concerning the extent of southern distinctiveness. First, there is the question of emphasis. Everyone can agree that in some ways the South resembled the North and in others it did not, but how does one determine whether it is more important that southerners and northerners had different labor systems, demographic patterns, and levels of urbanization or that they spoke the same language (more or less), belonged to the same religious denominations (more or less), and believed in the same constitution (more or less)? In his essay stressing the similarity between North and South, for example, Edward Pessen conceded, in passing, that "the striking similarities of the two antebellum sections of the nation neither erase their equally striking dissimilarities nor detract from the significance of these dissimilarities." Ticking off a lengthy list of contrasts, he suggested that "an essay focusing on these rather than on the themes emphasized here would highlight the vital disparities between the antebellum South and North." Then, however, he immediately reiterated his main point: "the antebellum North and South were far more alike than the conventional scholarly wisdom has led us to believe."[22] The comparativist needs to consider carefully which criteria should be used in establishing basic similarities and differences.

Second, scholars must come to grips with contextual variations. Here, two historical commonplaces work at cross purposes. If historians seek to understand a problem as contemporaries did, rather than "ahistorically" imposing on the past the values or perceptions of another time and place, they also believe that distance lends per-

---

labor, see Foner, *Free Soil, Free Labor, Free Men*, esp. chs. 1 and 2. For an effort to move beyond what he considers the outdated debate over slaveowners as paternalists versus slaveowners as capitalists by positing a "corporate individualism" under which antebellum masters embraced both market capitalism *and* an "organic" social order headed by benevolent slaveowner paternalists, see Jeffrey Robert Young, *Domesticating Slavery: The Master Class in Georgia and South Carolina, 1670–1837* (Chapel Hill: University of North Carolina Press, 1999). It is noteworthy, however, that Young does not confront the two very different understandings of *capitalism* underlying the interpretations he seeks to bridge; *his* capitalism is based on relations of exchange rather than of production.

22. Pessen, "How Different from Each Other Were the Antebellum North and South?" 1147.

spective and that hindsight affords the historian a crucial advantage over contemporaries in making sense of the past. Taken together, these two apparently contradictory assumptions show how context shapes historical judgment. The nearer one gets to something— geographically or temporally—the easier it is to recognize complexity and variation; the further one gets, the clearer the common patterns. To a late-twentieth-century Muslim cleric, the theological differences between southern and northern Baptists would appear insignificant, but to Baptists in antebellum America they loomed large. Similarly, a foreign observer (or one from a foreign century) would find it easier to perceive the common "Americanness" of antebellum northerners and southerners than would mid-nineteenth-century Americans caught up in the passions of the moment. It is therefore significant that so many foreign observers, even while seeking to explain what Americans shared in common, were struck by the differences between North and South. "The South is seceding from the North because the two are not homogeneous," wrote Englishman Anthony Trollope at the start of the Civil War. "They have different instincts, different appetites, different morals, and a different culture."[23] If such differences were apparent from afar, how much more pronounced must they have seemed to Americans themselves.

More common than broad societal comparisons have been those focusing on particular features of North and South. Historians have compared a variety of subjects across North-South lines—from economy, social structure, and political behavior to gender relations, family life, and social values—and even more await comparative study.[24] An examination of a specific comparison illustrates the practice and the promise of this kind of study.

23. Anthony Trollope, *North America,* ed. Robert Mason (1862; London: Penguin Books, 1992), 22. For a detailed examination of antebellum travel accounts, see Thomas D. Clark, ed., *Travels in the Old South: A Bibliography,* 3 vols. (Norman: University of Oklahoma Press, 1956).

24. See, for example, Fox-Genovese, *Within the Plantation Household*; Michael S. Hindus, *Prison and Plantation: Crime, Justice, and Authority in Massachusetts and South Carolina, 1767–1878* (Chapel Hill: University of North Carolina Press, 1980); Howard N. Rabinowitz, "A Comparative Perspective on Race Relations in Southern and Northern Cities, 1860–1900, with Special Emphasis on Raleigh, N.C.," in *Black Americans in North*

Few subjects have received as much comparative attention within the confines of one country as that of southern economic growth; indeed, this subject seems ready-made for comparative analysis. Not only is it highly quantifiable, but it is closely linked to the study of two topics of enduring historical interest: slavery and the Civil War. How better could one measure slavery's impact than by comparing the economic growth of the "slave" South and the "free" North? And how better measure the Civil War's impact than by evaluating the course of the South's postwar economic development?

Beginning in the 1960s, a widely (although not universally) shared consensus that slavery was a "backward" system that impeded southern economic growth was upset by a spate of econometric studies that reached full fruition in Robert W. Fogel and Stanley L. Engerman's *Time on the Cross* (1974) and Fogel's *Without Consent or Contract* (1989). Rebutting notions that the southern economy was stagnant and slavery increasingly unprofitable, these scholars stressed the Peculiar Institution's economic viability, suggested that slave-based agriculture was more productive than that using free labor, and argued that between 1840 and 1860 the southern economy grew faster than the northern. Such arguments were closely linked to—although analytically distinct from—the theme discussed above that slavery was a "highly developed form of capitalism" under which slaves were turned into "metaphorical clock punchers" who internalized the work ethic.[25]

Carolina and the South, ed. Jeffrey J. Crow and Flora J. Hatley (Chapel Hill: University of North Carolina Press, 1984), 137–59; William H. Pease and Jane H. Pease, *The Web of Progress: Private Values and Public Styles in Boston and Charleston, 1828–1843* (New York: Oxford University Press, 1985); Mark M. Smith, "Old South Time in Comparative Perspective," *American Historical Review* 101 (December 1996): 1432–69; John W. Quist, *Restless Visionaries: The Social Roots of Antebellum Reform in Alabama and Michigan* (Baton Rouge: Louisiana State University Press, 1998).

25. Alfred A. Conrad and John R. Meyer, "The Economics of Slavery in the Ante Bellum South," *Journal of Political Economy* 66 (1958): 95–130, and *The Economics of Slavery* (Chicago: Aldine Publishing Company, 1964); Fogel and Engerman, *Time on the Cross*; Fogel, *Without Consent or Contract* (quotations: 64, 162). For a recent work arguing for the increasing prevalence of modern "time consciousness" in the antebellum South, see Mark M. Smith, *Mastered by the Clock: Time, Slavery, and Freedom in the Antebellum South* (Chapel Hill: University of North Carolina Press, 1997). There is a huge critical literature discussing the recent debate over the economics of slavery; for my perspective, see Peter Kolchin, "Toward a Reinterpretation of Slavery," *Journal of Social His-*

Although most historians have accepted the conclusion that ante-bellum slavery was economically profitable, they have been less willing to buy the proposition that it in no way retarded or distorted southern economic development. To some extent, the apparently superior growth rate of the South reflected clever statistical manipulation, for Fogel and Engerman's own figures for per-capita income showed that although the southern economy as a whole was growing more rapidly than the northern, in every subregion of the South the growth rate was *slower* than in every subregion of the North, an anomaly caused by interregional population shifts:

	Per-Capita Income 1840	1860	Percentage annual increase
NORTH	$ 109	$ 141	1.3
Northeast	129	181	1.7
North Central	65	89	1.6
SOUTH	74	103	1.7
South Atlantic	66	84	1.2
East South Central	69	89	1.3
West South Central	151	184	1.0

More important, the southern economy was experiencing quantitative growth based on increased cultivation and export of staple crops (especially cotton) rather than the kind of qualitative transformation experienced by the northern economy during the late-antebellum years, and per-capita production figures masked a growing gap between the sections in aggregate production as population growth in the North sharply exceeded that in the South. Indeed, virtually every index of economic modernization *other* than per-capita growth—from urbanization and industrialization to mechanization,

tory 11 (Fall 1975): 99–113, and "More *Time on the Cross?* An Evaluation of Robert William Fogel's *Without Consent or Contract,*" *Journal of Southern History* 58 (August 1992): 491–502. On the *earlier* debate over the economics of slavery, see Harold D. Woodman, "The Profitability of Slavery: A Historical Perennial," *Journal of Southern History* 29 (1963): 303–25.

scientific endeavor, and education—indicated what contemporaries recognized: the antebellum South was lagging further and further behind the North. Fogel and his supporters tacitly acknowledged this lag, attributing the South's failure to urbanize and industrialize at the North's pace to the "comparative advantage" enjoyed by southern agriculture and the more elastic rural than urban demand for labor. At least, then, there is agreement that the southern economy was growing *differently* from that of the North.[26]

Much the same is true when it comes to analyzing the South's *post*war economic development. Belying widespread expectations of free-labor spokesmen that the destruction of slavery would usher in an era of southern prosperity, the South in many ways remained economically underdeveloped. Indeed, whereas in 1860 southern per-capita income stood at 80.5 percent of the national average, by 1880 it had plunged to 50.1 percent, a level that remained essentially unchanged over the next generation.[27]

26. The statistics on regional and subregional growth rates are from Fogel and Engerman, *Time on the Cross*, 248. For a few of the many challenges to this version of southern economic growth, see Harold D. Woodman, "Economic History and Economic Theory: The New Economic History in America," *Journal of Interdisciplinary History* 3 (Autumn 1972): 323–50; Gavin Wright, *The Political Economy of the Cotton South: Households, Markets, and Wealth in the Nineteenth Century* (New York: W. W. Norton, 1978); Fred Bateman and Thomas Weiss, *A Deplorable Scarcity: The Failure of Industrialization in the Slave Economy* (Chapel Hill: University of North Carolina Press, 1981), esp. 118–27, 157–63; and John Majewski, *A House Dividing: Economic Development in Pennsylvania and Virginia Before the Civil War* (New York: Cambridge University Press, 2000). The "comparative advantage" argument received full elaboration in Claudia Dale Goldin, *Urban Slavery in the American South, 1820–1860* (Chicago: University of Chicago Press, 1976). But for a still largely persuasive exposition of the basic contradiction between slavery and urban life, see Richard C. Wade, *Slavery in the Cities: The South, 1820–1860* (New York: Oxford University Press, 1964). This contradiction was noted at least as early as 1845, when Frederick Douglass observed that "[a] city slave is almost a freeman, compared with a slave on the plantation"; *Narrative of the Life of Frederick Douglass* (1845; New York: New American Library, 1968), 50.

27. Statistics are from Fogel, *Without Consent or Contract*, 89. As the persistence of this 50-percent level indicates, the southern economy, far from stagnating, grew at about the same pace as the northern during the last third of the nineteenth century, although from a lower base; what is more, between 1869 and 1899, *industrial* output in the ex-Confederate states grew at a faster pace than in the United States as a whole (7.8 percent versus 5.8 percent annually). See Gavin Wright, *Old South, New South: Revolutions in the Southern Economy Since the Civil War* (New York: Basic Books, 1986), 61.

An avalanche of historical writing has addressed the question of "what went wrong" in the postwar South, why the region suffered from continued poverty and exploitation rather than enjoying the free-labor paradise that many contemporaries and subsequent scholars felt "should" have emerged. If some scholars placed the blame on the tremendous destruction caused by the war,[28] two other explanations have been more common in recent years. Many social historians have ascribed continued backwardness to the failure to distribute land to former slaves and poor whites, and more generally to the failure to revolutionize the hierarchical, planter-dominated social structure. Economic historians, by contrast, have more often stressed the postbellum South's institutional imperfections. In one version, developed by Roger Ransom and Richard Sutch, "flawed economic institutions"—including a usurious credit system— combined with white racism to restrain southern development; in another, put forth by Gavin Wright, the South's "separate regional labor market" was the main culprit.[29]

I have questioned elsewhere the utility of this "tragic era" paradigm of the postwar South, with its emphasis on things gone wrong. For one thing, it is based on a tacit assumption that things usually go "right," that poverty, exploitation, and oppression are aberrations to be explained rather than normal features of human experience. For another, it is based on an implicit comparative judgment that developments in the South were *unusually* bleak, a judgment that I think does not stand up in comparison with other post-eman-

28. See, for example, James L. Sellers, "The Economic Incidence of the Civil War in the South," *Mississippi Valley Historical Review* 14 (September 1927): 179–91; E. Merton Coulter, *The South During Reconstruction, 1865–1877* (Baton Rouge: Louisiana State University Press, 1947), ch. 1; Fogel, *Without Consent or Contract*, 89. But for the argument that—as in most other modern wars—the *physical* damage wrought by the Civil War was quickly overcome, see Roger L. Ransom and Richard Sutch, *One Kind of Freedom: The Economic Consequences of Emancipation* (Cambridge, Eng.: Cambridge University Press, 1977), 40–55.

29. For the former approach, see Jonathan M. Wiener, *Social Origins of the New South: Alabama, 1860–1885* (Baton Rouge: Louisiana State University Press, 1978). For the latter, see Ransom and Sutch, *One Kind of Freedom* (quotation: 2); and Wright, *Old South, New South* (quotation: 7).

cipation societies.[30] Still, despite their differences over the reasons, most scholars have agreed that the postwar southern economy, like the prewar, followed a different course from that of the North. All of this suggests that what is at issue is less *whether* the South differed from the North than precisely how it did so, and why.

One of the most promising—but tricky—ways of grappling with southern distinctiveness involves exploring the elusive subject of southern identity. Of course, southerners (like everyone else) have felt numerous overlapping ties and loyalties: they have defined themselves in terms of their beliefs, values, associations, and occupations and have identified with others in terms of family, friendship, ethnicity, locality, region, and country. On the whole, however, it is safe to say that over the past century and a half, southerners have generally felt a stronger sense of regional attachment than most Americans. Local and national chauvinism may be prevalent virtually everywhere in America: people who live in grimy, polluted cities will enthusiastically rally around local sports teams and proudly proclaim that "we are number one," and residents of Iowa, Mississippi, and New Hampshire are all likely to defend the national honor by supporting air strikes on anyone who can conceivably be defined as threatening American interests. But aside from those who consider themselves southerners, most Americans have felt a relatively weak sense of regional loyalty; few people spend much time thinking of themselves as "midwesterners" or "mid-Atlantic-coasters." (The most notable exception to this generalization involves the American West; this exception suggests the utility of a historical comparison between South and West, a utility that has received some recognition among historians. Even westerners, however, have usually not invested the same symbolic meaning in their region that southerners have, no doubt in part because the West has lacked the kind of unifying experience that slavery and the Civil War provided for the South,

30. Peter Kolchin, "The Tragic Era? Interpreting Southern Reconstruction in Comparative Perspective," in *The Meaning of Freedom: Economics, Politics, and Culture After Slavery*, ed. Frank McGlynn and Seymour Drescher (Pittsburgh: University of Pittsburgh Press, 1992), 291–311.

and in part because most westerners are descended from easterners whereas most southerners are not descended from northerners.)[31]

Any such regional identification carries with it an implicit non-identification with what is outside the region, especially when regions are defined bipolarly, as South versus North. Being a southerner means being a non-Yankee. It does not, however, necessarily imply being a non-American. True, in one particular instance southernness *was* constructed in opposition to Americanness, and—because the Confederacy not only set itself up against the North but seceded from the United States—the distinction between "northern" and "American" as opposites of "southern" continued thereafter to be a tenuous one. Thus, in his 1974 book *The Americanization of Dixie: The Southernization of America,* John Egerton phrased his thesis not in terms of a growing convergence between South and North but as one between South and *America*: "The South is rushing to rejoin the Union," he wrote, "and in the process is becoming indistinguishable from the North and East and West." But more often, southerners have sharply distinguished between being un-northern and un-American. Indeed, according to a variety of indices, twentieth-century southerners have tended to be the *most* demonstratively patriotic of Americans, equating "military virtue with civic virtue," volunteering disproportionately for military service, supporting military action abroad more enthusiastically and less questioningly than other Americans, and objecting most strenuously to assaults on the national honor such as flag-burning or draft-

---

31. For the argument that the West, like the South, was a "constructed society" forged in the crucible of "cultural imperialism" from without, see David M. Emmons, "Constructed Province: History and the Making of the Last American West," *Western Historical Quarterly* 25 (Winter 1994): 437–59 (quotations: 442); for six critiques and Emmons's response, see ibid., 461–86. It is noteworthy that in outlining the "'top ten' reasons for treating the West as a region," Patricia Nelson Limerick focused on what *we* know about the West, with hindsight, rather than on the regional consciousness of westerners themselves; see her "Region and Reason," in Ayers et al., *All Over the Map*, 83–104 (quotation: 88). For an early effort at West-South comparison, see Douglas F. Dowd, "A Comparative Analysis of Economic Development in the American West and South," *Journal of Economic History* 16 (December 1956): 558–74. For a recent book that explores the intersection of South and West, see Neil Foley, *The White Scourge: Mexicans, Blacks, and Poor Whites in Texas Cotton Culture* (Berkeley: University of California Press, 1997).

dodging. What may at first glance seem a logical contradiction—identifying more strongly than most Americans at both the regional and national levels—is possible only by implicitly separating Americanness from Yankeeness: if self-identification as a southerner requires use of northerners as a negative reference group, the self-identification of southerner as American requires minimizing the Yankee nature of Americanness, even though *most* Americans are northerners.[32]

Because it necessitated a sudden redefinition of southern identity, emancipation—and the concurrent collapse of the Confederate effort to define a separate southern nationality—is especially useful in revealing this attempt to make "American" signify more than "northern," as well as the extent to which both southern and northern understandings of "the South" drew meaning only in terms of comparison with the North. What was at stake in the Reconstruction struggle was not only what it meant to be a southerner, but also what it meant to be an American. The shift from slave/Confederate South to free-labor/American South dictated redefinitions—among both northerners and southerners—of the South. For both, this process required coming to grips with the question of southerners' Americanness.

After the war, many northerners saw a bright future for a newly democratized South. Implicit in the free-labor critique of southern society that had come to prevail in the Republican Party was a highly contingent view of the South and southernness. To be sure, the in-

---

32. Egerton, *The Americanization of Dixie*, xix; Rod Andrew Jr., *Long Gray Lines: The Southern Military Tradition, 1839–1915* (Chapel Hill: University of North Carolina Press, 2001), 3. Both Carl N. Degler and Jack P. Greene have warned against assuming that a distinctive South implies a South that was outside the American mainstream: see Degler, "Thesis, Antithesis, Synthesis: The South, the North, and the Nation," *Journal of Southern History* 53 (February 1987): 3–18; and Greene, *Pursuits of Happiness: The Social Development of Early Modern British Colonies and the Formation of American Culture* (Chapel Hill: University of North Carolina Press, 1988). For an interesting example of a southern effort to identify the South with America and make a particular part of the North into the "other," see the recent account of a New York visitor to New Orleans, where the tour guide "asked everyone his or her place of origin," replying in each case "How nice! Welcome to New Orleans!" except to the New Yorker, to whom he replied "Welcome to America"; "Metropolitan Diary," *New York Times*, 13 March 2000, A22.

grained free-labor image of the South as a backward, impoverished, and degraded region was highly negative and has usually been considered "antisouthern." But the South was not *inherently* backward, impoverished, and degraded according to this view; it was slavery that had made it so. "It was necessary that I should travel to Virginia to have any idea of a slave State," declared William H. Seward. "An exhausted soil, old and decaying towns, wretchedly-neglected roads, and, in every respect, an absence of enterprise and improvement, distinguish the region. . . . Such has been the effect of slavery." Implicit in the notion that slavery was responsible for the defective character of the antebellum South was the assumption that the abolition of slavery would make possible—indeed, almost inevitable— the rapid regeneration of the once benighted region.[33]

Indeed, although wartime passions sometimes got the better of them, most thoughtful and articulate Republicans shied away from the position that the South was intrinsically un-American. One way they were able to do this, even while whipping up hostility to the Confederacy, was to maintain that only a minority of disloyal activists—the notorious "slave power" conspirators—were responsible for the rebellion. Just as Abraham Lincoln and other Republicans had denounced the efforts of a few troublemakers to hoodwink the southern majority before the war, so too the persistent wartime efforts to set up Unionist governments within the South under the leadership of "loyal" southerners were predicated on the assumption that most southerners wanted to be good Americans, and would be under the right circumstances; perhaps the most tenuous—but ideologically significant—of these efforts was the Lincoln Administration's recognition of the Alexandria-based administration-in-exile led by Governor Francis H. Pierpont as the legitimate government of Virginia (a policy in some ways reminiscent of the later American recognition of the Nationalist Chinese regime on Taiwan as the government of China). The idea of a "slave power conspiracy" also un-

33. The classic study of the free-labor ideology is Foner, *Free Soil, Free Labor, Free Men;* see esp. 40–72 for the free-labor critique of the South, and 41 for the Seward quotation. For emphasis on the "antisouthern" nature of northern ideology in the late antebellum period, see Grant, *North Over South.*

dergirded the position of Andrew Johnson, himself a loyal southerner—that is, loyal to the Union—who upon his accession to the presidency blamed haughty aristocrats for the Confederate rebellion and based his restoration policy on the presumed loyalty of ordinary southerners.[34]

Thus, with the defeat of the Confederacy and the abolition of slavery, many northerners found it easy to contemplate a happy and prosperous future for a South that would be transformed by the magic of free labor—plus northern determination to pursue war aims to their logical conclusion. Indiana Congressman George W. Julian, one of the most fervent of northern Radicals, expressed this view nicely in contrasting the old South, with its "large estates, widely scattered settlements, wasteful agriculture, popular ignorance, social degradation, the decline of manufactures, contempt for honest labor, and a pampered oligarchy," with his vision for what the new South could be, a land of "small farms, thrifty tillage, free schools, social independence, flourishing manufactures and the arts, respect for honest labor, and equality of political rights." Although northerners held widely varying views of precisely what should be done with the defeated South, most were convinced that if the right decisions were made—and this is what Reconstruction was all about—the very nature of the South would be miraculously trans-

34. On Republicans' exaggeration of southern Unionism during the secession crisis, see David M. Potter, *Lincoln and His Party During the Secession Crisis* (New Haven: Yale University Press, 1942). For a study that gives a new twist to the "slave power" thesis, by emphasizing the complicity of "Doughfaces" (northerners who supported prosouthern policies) in maintaining slaveholders' hegemony, see Leonard L. Richards, *The Slave Power: The Free North and Southern Dominion, 1780–1860* (Baton Rouge: Louisiana State University Press, 2000); for a very different approach, see David Brion Davis, *The Slave Power Conspiracy and the Paranoid Style* (Baton Rouge: Louisiana State University Press, 1969). Even children's literature in the wartime North emphasized the "slave power" theme; see James Marten, *The Children's Civil War* (Chapel Hill: University of North Carolina Press, 1998), 41–42. On Andrew Johnson's class-based view of southern loyalty, see Du Bois, *Black Reconstruction in America*, 237–334; Eric L. McKitrick, *Andrew Johnson and Reconstruction* (Chicago: University of Chicago Press, 1959), 85–92, 139–40; and Kenneth M. Stampp, *The Era of Reconstruction, 1865–1877* (New York: Vintage Books, 1965), 50–82. On the Pierpont government, see Charles H. Ambler, *Francis H. Pierpont: Union War Governor of Virginia and Father of West Virginia* (Chapel Hill: University of North Carolina Press, 1937).

formed. In short, the Reconstruction South was a new frontier, making possible the fulfillment of American aspirations; in becoming Americans once again, southerners would also come to resemble northerners.[35]

Although some former Confederates, too, got carried away with their emotions, the vast majority of those who were politically active also insisted on their Americanness. They pursued a variety of tactics, but these generally were predicated on an implicit rejection of Confederate nationality and assertion of their existing American citizenship. If many northerners saw the need to make southerners true Americans as justifying prescriptive Reconstruction policies, the typical response of white southerners was to argue that because they already were true Americans, no federal action was needed. Facilitating this response was the widespread conviction in the wartime South that it was the *Confederates* who were upholding basic American principles dating back to the War for Independence and that it was the North's "Black Republicans" who were undermining those principles—and the United States Constitution. In a curious way, emancipation served to promote the American identity of southerners, for to the extent that Confederate nationalism was rooted in a commitment to slavery, its abolition made possible a renewed emphasis on shared American values.[36]

The switch from being good Confederates to good Americans

---

35. For Julian's remarks of 17 November 1865, see Michael Les Benedict, ed., *The Fruits of Victory: Alternatives in Restoring the Union, 1865–1877* (Philadelphia: J. B. Lippincott Company, 1975), 93–94. On the northern postwar vision of a free-labor South—and the growing disenchantment with this ideal—see Heather Cox Richardson, *The Death of Reconstruction: Race, Labor, and Politics in the Post-Civil War North, 1865–1901* (Cambridge, Mass.: Harvard University Press, 2001).

36. The presence of slavery "made Southerners believe that they constituted a separate nation" even though in reality southerners and northerners shared "intellectual, political, social, and economic beliefs" and therefore did not constitute "two distinct peoples," argued John McCardell in *The Idea of a Southern Nation*, 3–4. Although McCardell's suggestion that southerners did not objectively form a nation or people is problematical, because *nation* and *people* are themselves subjective concepts based on perceived identity, his emphasis on slavery as the driving force behind (white) southern nationalism is persuasive. For more on Confederate nationalism, see below, Chapter 3, pp. 88–93.

was astonishingly rapid. "I regard the contest at an end," declared former Confederate Congressman and General Howell Cobb of Georgia; urging the federal government to restore previous political relations as quickly as possible, he called on ex-Confederates to pursue "a return to the peaceful and quiet employment of life; obedience to the constitution and laws of the United States." Former Confederate Vice President Alexander Stephens agreed, telling the Joint Committee on Reconstruction that "towards the Constitution of the United States the great mass of our people were always as much devoted in their feelings as any people ever were towards any laws or people" and urging "an immediate restoration, an immediate bringing back of the States into their original practical relations." As historian Thomas G. Dyer has recently pointed out, at the war's end "Southerners constructed revisionist accounts of their own prewar and wartime activities, a reconstruction of loyalty that continued throughout 1865 and 1866. . . . This logic enabled all but a few to claim that they had been Unionists, loyal adherents to the United States either before the war or at some point during the war." Significantly, this revisionist position was remarkably close to Andrew Johnson's: from both Johnson's perspective and that of many former Confederates, because southerners were just as much Americans as New Yorkers or Ohioans, any further reconstruction of their states was not only unnecessary but unconstitutional. The new southern orthodoxy also bore a noteworthy—although usually unnoted—similarity to the "slave power conspiracy" doctrine that had, at least in its more moderate versions, implicitly distinguished between the loyal mass of southerners and a small group of traitorous leaders.[37]

37. The Cobb and Stephens quotations are from Walter L. Fleming, ed., *Documentary History of Reconstruction: . . . 1865–1906,* 2 vols. (1897; New York: McGraw-Hill Book Company, 1966), I, 128, 235; for the Dyer quotation, see Thomas G. Dyer, *Secret Yankees: The Union Circle in Confederate Atlanta* (Baltimore: Johns Hopkins University Press, 1999), 219. See William A. Dunning, *Essays on the Civil War and Reconstruction* (1897; New York: Harper & Row, 1965), 101–105; McKitrick, *Andrew Johnson and Reconstruction,* 96; and Michael Perman, *Reunion Without Compromise: The South and Reconstruction, 1865–1868* (Cambridge, Eng.: Cambridge University Press, 1973), 30–39. Johnson's position differed from that of most former Confederates in that he conceded to the Federal government the right to impose three conditions on the southern states: abolition of slavery, repudiation of secession, and repudiation of Confederate war debts. On conflict-

I shall examine in chapters 2 and 3 some of the implications that such views held for Confederate nationalism, but what is noteworthy for consideration here is the distinction that former Confederates drew—were forced to draw—between Americanness and Yankeeness. If northern Republicans, in charting an "American" path for their erstwhile enemies, saw this path as leading in a northerly direction, the ex-Confederates, in insisting that they had been good Americans all along, had a very different conception of what such Americanness meant; certainly, it did *not* mean that they were—or would become—essentially Yankees. As late as May 1866, for example, Mary Jones, widow of the prominent Georgia Presbyterian minister Charles C. Jones, was still referring to "wicked Yankees," even though eight months earlier she had joined other southern "aristocrats" in swearing allegiance to the United States and its Constitution. If during the war Mrs. Jones had proclaimed that "every development of [i.e., experience with] the enemy but confirms my desire for a separate and distinct nationality," after the war, as her world collapsed around her, she found it easy to revert to American nationality even while bitterly bemoaning the suffering she endured at the hands of northern aggression.[38]

Toward the end of the war, a young planter in Georgia expressed his undying hatred for "the accursed Yankee nation": "I have vowed," he wrote, "that if I ever have children—the first ingredient of the first principle of their education shall be uncompromising hatred & contempt of the Yankee." After the war, although such open

---

ing theories of Reconstruction, see Michael Les Benedict, *A Compromise of Principle: Congressional Republicans and Reconstruction, 1863–1869* (New York: W. W. Norton, 1974); and Foner, *Reconstruction,* esp. 228–80.

38. Mary Jones to her daughter Mary Ruth Jones, 18 May 1866; Jones oath of allegiance, 8 September 1865; Jones journal entry, 17 January 1865, in *The Children of Pride: A True Story of Georgia and the Civil War,* ed. Robert Manson Myers (New Haven: Yale University Press, 1972), 1336, 1296, 1247. Noting that "Reason" had been "dethroned" in "our beloved South," Jones's son Charles C. Jones Jr. proclaimed that "no one will wish to be there who can reside elsewhere" and moved to New York to pursue business interests and practice law. Advising his mother to "sell out all the stock and perishable property at Montevideo and rent the place if a responsible person presents himself," he urged her to abandon the family plantation and divide her time with her children. Charles S. Jones Jr. to Mary Jones, 30 October 1867, Myers, ed., *Children of Pride,* 1402–3.

expressions of animosity became less common (both because they were impolitic and because the intensity of war-generated hatreds gradually faded), former Confederates continued to stress the distinction between themselves and their conquerors, whom they continued to view as unsouthern and uncivilized. During his extensive travels through the postwar South, journalist Whitelaw Reid found that southern whites, failing to recognize him as a northerner, would over and over spontaneously offer their low opinion of Yankees; "the burden of all their discourse," he reported, "was the meanness, the ignorance, the hatefulness, the cowardice of the detested Yankees."[39]

Anger, bitterness, humiliation, and hatred of Yankees were fundamental staples of the postwar South, evident in the widespread hostility directed at northerners who came south. Northerners with political messages—"carpetbaggers" and teacher/missionaries—were the most conspicuous targets of this hostility, but as Lawrence Powell has shown, those who came south to invest were by no means immune. And even as wartime hostilities gradually faded and ex-Confederates embraced what Nina Silber has termed the "romance of reunion," the term *Yankee* retained for most southern whites its sharply negative connotations, a synonym for pushy, aggressive, insensitive, opportunistic, and mercenary. By contrast, in their *self*-representations reflected in Lost-Cause celebrations of the Confederacy, as Gaines Foster has shown, white southerners emphasized very different traits—"order, deference to authority, and tradition"—and in the process "helped imbue the New South with values and attitudes that rendered it a particularly conservative society." In short, after the war, as before, conceptualizing the South required an implicit contrast with an un-South, although that un-South was itself a variable construct that depending on its definition could serve divergent purposes. Indeed, despite northern predictions of a northern-oriented—American—path for the postwar South, the Civil War led to a strengthened rather a diminished

39. Quotations are from Roark, *Masters Without Slaves,* 86; and Whitelaw Reid, *After the War: A Tour of the Southern States, 1865–1866,* ed. C. Vann Woodward (1866; New York: Harper Torchbooks, 1965), 441.

sense of southern distinctiveness. The southern political system, to take one example, diverged from the national norm far more sharply after the war—whether during Reconstruction or the subsequent era that culminated in the emergence of a "solid South"—than it had during the antebellum years.[40]

If most southerners now agreed on their Americanness, they disagreed sharply among themselves over what this meant—and therefore over what being southern meant. Indeed, such disagreement was endemic to the process of southern self-identification for the simple reason that there were so many different kinds of southerners. Clearly there was not *one* South but *many* Souths. That is the subject of chapter 2.

40. The quotation is from Gaines M. Foster, *Ghosts of the Confederacy: Defeat, the Lost Cause, and the Emergence of the New South* (New York: Oxford University Press, 1987), 195. See Lawrence N. Powell, *New Masters: Northern Planters During the Civil War and Reconstruction* (New Haven: Yale University Press, 1980), esp. 55–72, 123–33; and Nina Silber, *The Romance of Reunion: Northerners and the South, 1865–1900* (Chapel Hill: University of North Carolina Press, 1993). On the war's creation of a heightened sense of southernness, see Goldfield, *Still Fighting the Civil War*.

2   MANY SOUTHS

In chapter 1, I considered the South in an American context, arguing that conceptualizing the South has inevitably involved making implicit comparisons between it and what I termed the "un-South," that is, the North. Here, I want to address a second—internal—kind of comparison among the region's various components that constituted, in effect, "many Souths." Once again, I shall consider how historians have approached this kind of comparison, both explicitly and implicitly, and how I think they might profitably do so in the future. My point of departure is the simple premise that defining and describing the South involves establishing not just how it has differed from the rest of the country, but also how much cohesion and variation have existed within its borders. In what sense should a suburb of Washington, D.C., be regarded as part of the same section as a suburb of New Orleans? If a southern "drawl" can be recognized as distinct from accents found in Philadelphia, Boston, or New York, what unites the English spoken in southern Louisiana, tidewater Virginia, lowcounty South Carolina, and upcountry Georgia and makes them all recognizable as "southern"? Clearly, there have been and continue to be many Souths.

The most obvious (although not necessarily the most important) form of variation within the South is geographical. Scholars have long recognized (and criticized others for failing to recognize) that the South was far from a monolithic region, even if they have not always agreed on how to divide it.[1] Just as one can compare the

---

1. "My chief objection to previous accounts of the South, including my own, is that portraits tend to flatten out the rich variety of southern types," wrote William W. Freehling. "[C]hange was omnipresent, varieties abounded, visions multiplied." Freehling, *The Road to Disunion: Secessionists at Bay, 1776–1854* (New York: Oxford University Press, 1990), vii. Even W. J. Cash, who stressed a southern unity so all-encompassing that one

South with the North, so too one can compare subregions of the South with each other: Upper versus Lower South, seaboard versus inland, blackbelt versus upcountry. One can also narrow the focus further and make comparisons within a particular subregion or state: between southern versus northern Louisiana, for example, or among Mobile, New Orleans, and Galveston as Gulf Coast cities. And as with North-South comparisons, internal comparisons can be of geographic subregions as generalized entities or of particular events, institutions, and processes within these subregions—for example, comparing slavery in the Upper and Lower Souths, or the economic growth of the cotton and tobacco Souths, or Reconstruction in Georgia and South Carolina. The possibilities are practically endless.

Two recent prize-winning books on slavery illustrate some of the opportunities afforded by such internal comparison. In *Many Thousands Gone: The First Two Centuries of Slavery in North America,* Ira Berlin provides a sweeping survey of slavery in four regions of colonial and Revolutionary-era North America: the Chesapeake, the South Carolina and Georgia lowcountry, the Lower Mississippi Valley, and the North. Although the book is in some ways a series of juxtaposed "parallel" histories and much of the comparison is implicit rather than explicit, comparative themes inevitably emerge as Berlin develops the ways in which his four regions experienced common trends even as specific historical conditions shaped variations among them. Each southern region, for example, went through three distinct eras, progressing from a "society with slaves" (that is, in which some slaves were present) to a true "slave society" (in which the social order was based on slavery) and then facing a challenge to slavery in the Revolutionary era. But this chronological progression unfolded differently in each region, in terms of both timing and the particular social relations that ensued; the Revolutionary-era challenge to slavery, for example, produced markedly different results in the various regions.[2]

---

could speak of a homogenized southern "mind," noted the existence of "many Souths"; see his *The Mind of the South* (New York: Alfred A. Knopf, Inc., 1941), viii.

2. Ira Berlin, *Many Thousands Gone: The First Two Centuries of Slavery in North America* (Cambridge, Mass.: Harvard University Press, 1998).

More explicitly comparative is Philip D. Morgan's *Slave Counterpoint: Black Culture in the Eighteenth-Century Chesapeake and Lowcountry*. Rather than examining slavery in all of the North American mainland, Morgan limits his focus to the two most important slave societies on the English mainland, in each chapter engaging in carefully crafted historical comparison. Lacking the dynamic sweep of Berlin's volume, Morgan's almost encyclopedic study offers in its stead a nuanced delineation of the similarities and differences between two evolving slave societies—lowcountry slaves were typically less healthy than their Chesapeake counterparts, for example, but enjoyed greater autonomy—in the process providing an authoritative statement of our current understanding of slavery in the colonial South.[3]

Although many people—perhaps conditioned by decades of "compare and contrast" exam questions—assume that comparison inevitably involves *two* items, such a binary structure is by no means an essential component of comparison. Indeed, in order to form meaningful generalizations, it is clearly preferable to have more than two cases on which to base one's judgments. Because they are especially demanding in terms of expertise and research, however, multi-case comparisons have typically found less favor among historians than among sociologists, who are less fanatical about the need to base findings on primary sources. One thinks, for example, of Orlando Patterson's wide-ranging survey, *Slavery and Social Death*, which examines slavery in sixty-six slave societies across time and space.[4] But if few historians are brave—or foolhardy—enough to attempt such an all-encompassing study, the multicase historical comparison lives in edited collections with contributions by several authors, each of whom sketches a portion of the broader historical picture. In a recent book entitled *The Freedmen's Bureau and Re-*

3. Philip D. Morgan, *Slave Counterpoint: Black Culture in the Eighteenth-Century Chesapeake and Lowcountry* (Chapel Hill: University of North Carolina Press, 1998).

4. Orlando Patterson, *Slavery and Social Death: A Comparative Study* (Cambridge, Mass.: Harvard University Press, 1982). For a fine historical study that moves beyond traditional two-case comparison by focusing on three geographic areas of the South, see J. William Harris, *Deep Souths: Delta, Piedmont, and Sea Island Society in the Age of Segregation* (Baltimore: Johns Hopkins University Press, 2001).

construction, edited by Paul A. Cimbala and Randall M. Miller, thirteen authors examine the operations of the Freedmen's Bureau in ten different states or localities—ranging from Maryland to New Orleans—with separate chapters also exploring the Bureau's relationship with Andrew Johnson, Ulysses S. Grant, and the Southern Homestead Act. Such a volume cannot be fully comparative: indeed, with the exception of Miller's useful introductory overview, most of the essays are not comparative at all. Still, by juxtaposing the experiences of the Freedmen's Bureau in diverse states, this book allows the *reader* both to note differences and to form generalizations, and thus provides an important first step toward a multifaceted historical comparison.[5]

At the opposite extreme, a very different sort of comparison is evident in a type of history that is usually not considered comparative at all: local history. Because any history of a small geographic unit inevitably raises questions of typicality, it is implicitly comparative. Noting the distinctiveness of an area that James C. Cobb characterized as "the most southern place on earth," John C. Willis has recently suggested that the Mississippi Delta "may best reveal the cotton South through contrast." Because "the Delta's history seldom corresponded with the chronologies of the rest of the postbellum South"—still largely a "wilderness" except for its River plantations in 1865, it offered unusual opportunities for former slaves during the first generation of freedom and became a "thoroughly repressive society" only after the turn of the twentieth century, "a decade later and with much greater economic and physical violence" than in most of the South—the area's "frequent disjunctures cast the larger region in relief." In this kind of study, a locality's significance can stem from its very atypicality, and the *least* typical case can be analytically the most useful.[6]

5. Paul A. Cimbala and Randall M. Miller, eds., *The Freedmen's Bureau and Reconstruction: Reconsiderations* (New York: Fordham University Press, 1999). Many conferences, and conference sessions, are comparative in precisely this sense. By bringing together and juxtaposing multiple case studies, they enable the audience—sometimes aided by commentators—to engage in their own comparison. At the very least, therefore, they promote comparative *consciousness* among historians.

6. John C. Willis, *Forgotten Time: The Yazoo-Mississippi Delta After the Civil War* (Charlottesville: University Press of Virginia, 2000), 4; James C. Cobb, *The Most Southern Place on Earth: The Mississippi Delta and the Roots of Southern Identity* (New York: Oxford University Press, 1992).

Take, for example, the history of the most border of border states: tiny Delaware. Every state to its north abolished slavery during the late eighteenth and early nineteenth centuries; in every state to its south, a significant proportion of the population remained enslaved down to the Civil War. But Delaware followed neither the southern nor the northern pattern: by 1860, the state's 1,798 slaves constituted less than 2 percent of its population and less than 10 percent of its black population; it had become practically a free state. Nevertheless, Delaware's lawmakers stubbornly refused to abolish slavery, even when offered the possibility of compensated emancipation during the Civil War, and after the war they refrained from ratifying the Thirteenth Amendment to the Constitution until 1901. Any examination of the history of slavery in Delaware of necessity becomes an exercise in comparative history, an attempt to explain why the state followed the course that it did instead of that pursued either to the north or the south.[7]

As such geographical variations suggest, historians seeking to come to grips with the nature and distinctiveness of the South must also consider whether one can differentiate degrees of southernness. Most people would agree that border states (such as Delaware) are in some ways southern and in some ways not. Whether one is struck more by the presence or absence of their southernness is likely to depend heavily on one's frame of reference: what appears southern to an observer from Connecticut may not to one from Mississippi. But can we also talk about being more or less southern within what everyone would accept as the South? Should we regard the Deep South as more southern than the Upper South? Terming the Mississippi Delta "the most southern place on earth" clearly implies that

7. Two recent books trace the peculiar history of the Peculiar Institution in Delaware: William H. Williams, *Slavery and Freedom in Delaware, 1639–1865* (Wilmington, Del.: Scholarly Resources, 1996); and Patience Essah, *A House Divided: Slavery and Emancipation in Delaware, 1638–1865* (Charlottesville: University Press of Virginia, 1996). For the argument that "the development of slavery in Texas between 1836 and 1861 was quite different from the simultaneous history of slavery in any other contemporary slave state" and that "it is precisely those differences that make Texas a revealing location for an exploration of slavery and slave resistance," see William Dean Carrigan, "Slavery on the Frontier: The Peculiar Institution in Central Texas," *Slavery and Abolition* 20 (August 1999): 63–96 (quotation: 64).

one can grade locations on their degree of southernness, creating a hierarchy ranging from most to least southern. But according to what criteria? The grits line? The presence of sweet (iced) tea? Cotton? Use of *y'all* as the plural form of *you*? In an updated version of Jefferson's geographic gradation, William W. Freehling observed that "the further north the southern state, the cooler the clime, the fewer the slaves, and the lower the relative commitment to perpetuating bondage." To the extent that slavery and the Civil War shaped the nineteenth-century South, one could suggest a ranking of southernness based on secession behavior, with South Carolina the most southern state, followed by six Deep South states, four Upper South states, the border states, the southernmost free states, and finally the northern tier of states in New England and the upper Midwest.[8] (One could further subdivide individual states, categorizing western Tennessee and southern Delaware as more southern than eastern Tennessee and northern Delaware.) Of course, any attempt to measure degrees of southernness must inevitably be a subjective exercise that will provoke not only disagreement over what criteria should be used but also unhappiness over being judged *too* southern or not southern *enough*. Clearly, however, it is necessary to come to grips with *different* Souths, whether or not one sees fit to rank them as more and less southern.

A second form of internal variation within the South involves change over time. Indeed, the very notion of what is southern is subject to change. Most historians would categorize eighteenth-century Maryland as southern; few Americans today consider Maryland part of the South, and the Census Bureau typically labels it as "Mid-Atlantic." Even within the Deep South, the nature of southernness has been subject to change, as is suggested in the title of Christopher Morris's book on Warren County, Mississippi: *Becoming Southern*. Only gradually, Morris argues in his opening paragraph, did the county's residents "develop a way of life that contemporary Americans and later historians identified as South-

---

8. Freehling, *The Road to Disunion,* 17. On the convergence of slaveholding and secession as criteria for southernness, see above, chapter 1, page 16.

ern." Of course, embodied in this argument is an implicit definition of what it meant to be southern, but for my purposes here, what is noteworthy in Morris's formulation is the developmental nature of southernness. The South is not so much a place as a way of behaving that continually evolved.[9]

Of course, in one sense, all history involves comparison over time. But just as the attempt to make variations over space explicit can turn noncomparative into comparative history, so too can conscious attention to change over time. It has been a commonplace, for example, that most studies of antebellum slavery provide what is essentially a "snapshot" of the last (atypical) years of the Peculiar Institution rather than tracing the ways in which it changed—and didn't change—over the generations. Colonial-era slavery differed from its antebellum descendant in areas as varied as demography, family life, slaveowner ideology, and master-slave relations. To take one obvious example, although historians have properly emphasized the role that Christianity played in the late-antebellum slave quarters, the conversion of the slaves did not reach notable proportions until the late eighteenth and early nineteenth centuries; as Philip Morgan put it, "the vast majority of eighteenth-century Anglo-American slaves lived and died strangers to Christianity." Because most of the slave sources we have date from the late-antebellum period, those sources have tended to dominate the historical recreation of slavery in America. It is therefore important to emphasize that the slavery described in those sources was not necessarily the slavery that existed for most of the Peculiar Institution's two-hundred-and-fifty-year history.[10]

9. Christopher Morris, *Becoming Southern: The Evolution of a Way of Life, Warren County and Vicksburg, Mississippi, 1770–1860* (New York: Oxford University Press, 1995), vii. On the evolving "southernness" of northeast Texas, see Walter L. Buenger, *The Path to a Modern South: Northeast Texas Between Reconstruction and the Great Depression* (Austin: University of Texas Press, 2001), and Buenger's e-mail clarification to H-SOUTH@H-NET.MSU.EDU (22 July 2002): "From 1820 to 1910 Texas grew more like the South. From 1910 to 1930 a subtle transformation began. Since 1930 Texas has grown less like the South."

10. Morgan, *Slave Counterpoint,* 420. On the centrality of Christianity to antebellum slave life, see, inter alia, Eugene D. Genovese, *Roll, Jordan, Roll: The World the Slaves Made* (New York: Pantheon, 1974), esp. 161–284; and John B. Boles, ed., *Masters & Slaves*

There are at least two ways in which scholars can focus on change over time. The most common is to study a subject over a broad chronological span; this is the approach that I took, for example, in my book *American Slavery, 1619–1877,* which traces the Peculiar Institution's evolution from its establishment through its abolition and the post-emancipation struggle over Reconstruction.[11] More explicitly comparative is a second, rarely employed approach involving comparison of a particular item in two different chronological eras—for example, Chesapeake slavery (or social structure, or political ideology) in the mid-eighteenth century with that in the mid-nineteenth century. This second approach, which is just as truly comparative as is comparison over space, strikes me as especially promising, and I believe that its application could make important contributions to our understanding of a wide range of historical problems.

A central preoccupation of many southern historians—grappling with the perennial question of change versus continuity—is implicitly comparative in the sense that I have just been discussing. Although the dichotomy is too neat and obscures a range of positions in between, historians have divided into two camps, one of which emphasizes elements of continuity in southern history and the other sharp turning-points or discontinuities. Those falling into the first camp have varied, of course, over precisely what it was that provided the basis for southern continuity; two well-known versions included emphasis by U. B. Phillips on white supremacy and by W. J. Cash on a premodern "mind." On the other side, C. Vann Woodward lobbied strenuously against the notion of a monolithic, unchanging South, pointing to the sharp break between the Old South and the New and arguing that the supposedly time-honored southern tradition of racial segregation was in fact largely a product of the 1890s and the early years of the twentieth century. (Howard N. Rabinowitz has noted the announcement of at least three "New Souths" since 1920, in addition to the most commonly cited "first" New

---

in the House of the Lord: Race and Religion in the American South, 1740–1870 (Lexington: University Press of Kentucky, 1988).

11. Peter Kolchin, *American Slavery, 1619–1877* (New York: Hill & Wang, 1993).

South of 1877–1919.) Significant ideological implications typically underlay these disagreements: the practical corollary of Woodward's thesis, for example, was that because segregation was not a long-standing, immutable southern institution, its abolition would not be as difficult as many people were suggesting.[12]

More recently, historians have engaged in an intense debate over how "revolutionary" the Civil War, emancipation, and Reconstruction were, with some such as Jonathan M. Wiener and Jay Mandle stressing the basic elements of continuity between the Old South and the New, and others such as Eric Foner and Barbara Fields describing a bourgeois revolution that led to a halting, uneven, but unstoppable transformation of a slaveholding into a capitalistic society.[13] Any effort to come to grips with the impact of the Civil War and Reconstruction—whether in broad systemic terms or more narrowly focused on specific themes such as the condition of the freed slaves—must be at least implicitly comparative, because determining

12. Ulrich B. Phillips, "The Central Theme of Southern History," *American Historical Review* 34 (1928): 30–43; Cash, *The Mind of the South*; C. Vann Woodward, *Origins of the New South, 1877–1913* (Baton Rouge: Louisiana State University Press, 1951), and Woodward, *The Strange Career of Jim Crow* (New York: Oxford University Press, 1955 and subsequent editions); Howard N. Rabinowitz, *The First New South, 1865–1920* (Arlington Heights, Ill.: Harlan Davidson, 1992), 1–2. For an insightful analysis of Woodward's evolving thought on segregation, see Howard N. Rabinowitz, "More Than the Woodward Thesis: Assessing *The Strange Career of Jim Crow*," *Journal of American History* 75 (December 1988): 842–56.

13. For examples of work emphasizing continuity, see Carl N. Degler, *Place Over Time: The Continuity of Southern Distinctiveness* (Baton Rouge: Louisiana State University Press, 1977); Jonathan M. Wiener, *Social Origins of the New South: Alabama, 1860–1885* (Baton Rouge: Louisiana State University Press, 1978); and Jay R. Mandle, *The Roots of Black Poverty: The Southern Plantation Economy After the Civil War* (Durham: Duke University Press, 1978), reissued with slight revisions as *Not Slave, Not Free: The African-American Economic Experience Since the Civil War* (Durham: Duke University Press, 1992). Among the many works emphasizing "transformation" are Eric Foner, *Reconstruction: America's Unfinished Revolution, 1863–1877* (New York: Harper & Row, 1988); and Barbara Jeanne Fields, "The Advent of Capitalist Agriculture: The New South in a Bourgeois World," in *Essays on the Postbellum Southern Economy*, ed. Thavolia Glymph and John J. Kushma (College Station: Texas A&M University Press, 1985), 73–94. For discussion of some of these issues, see Peter Kolchin, "Slavery and Freedom in the Civil War South," in *Writing the Civil War: The Quest to Understand*, ed. James M. McPherson and William J. Cooper Jr. (Columbia: University of South Carolina Press, 1998), esp. 254–57.

their impact makes sense only in terms of what had existed before. Here, once again, the temporal perspective of the viewer is crucial. For example, if judging Reconstruction from the standpoint of the late twentieth (or early twenty-first) century suggests that not enough was done to provide the former slaves with full equality—thereby implicitly emphasizing continuity—from the vantage point of 1859 a very different judgment—accentuating change— would be in order: on the eve of the Civil War, virtually no one predicted that within a decade not only would slavery be abolished but former slaves would be going to school, voting, and serving on juries.[14]

A third, and in some ways the most important, kind of variation within the South is that among groups of southerners, whether those groups are defined in ideological, ethnic, cultural, or class terms. Despite the proclivity of many people to think in stereotypical terms—it is hard, for example, to break students of the habit of reifying regions, saying "the South felt" this or "the North wanted" that——the protypical southerner does not exist. In grappling with the "character" of the South, one must continually confront the question of *which* southerners one is considering, or who represents the South.

Perhaps the clearest enunciation of this simple point is to be found in a book called *The Other South,* in which Carl N. Degler focused on those he termed the "losers" who dissented from the South's dominant ethos—southern whites who opposed slavery, remained Unionists during the Civil War, and sought to forge a more egalitarian society in the late nineteenth century.[15] Although Degler's "other southerners" were limited to whites who questioned prevailing norms concerning race and slavery, there are many other notable variations: over the centuries, southerners have included women as well as men, blacks as well as whites, poor whites as well

14. For elaboration of this point, see Peter Kolchin, "The Tragic Era? Interpreting Southern Reconstruction in Comparative Perspective," in *The Meaning of Freedom: Economics, Politics, and Culture After Slavery,* ed. Frank McGlynn and Seymour Drescher (Pittsburgh: University of Pittsburgh Press, 1992), esp. 297–300.

15. Carl N. Degler, *The Other South: Southern Dissenters in the Nineteenth Century* (New York: Harper & Row, 1974), 1 (quotation).

as yeoman farmers and planters, immigrants, mechanics, Jews, socialists, populists, racists, democrats (both with capital and small *d*),
republicans (with capital and small *r*), shopkeepers, accountants,
Cajuns, secretaries, waiters, conservatives, domestic servants, liberals, Catholics, Baptists, soldiers, teachers, airline pilots, Hispanics,
and prostitutes—and that is just a start. To generalize about the
southernness of these southerners is indeed a herculean task.

Historians of the South have in recent years devoted considerable—and growing—effort to exploring variations according to sex,
as southern women finally receive the historical attention that so long
eluded them. These historians have by no means achieved interpretive unity: among other divisions, perhaps the most fundamental remains that between scholars such as Elizabeth Fox-Genovese, who
have seen southern women's lives as fundamentally different from
those of their northern sisters, and those such as Suzanne Lebsock
and Elizabeth Varon, who have been more impressed by their similar
experiences, values, and endeavors. (This division reflects, of course,
the basic disagreement discussed in chapter 1 over the degree of
southern distinctiveness.) Indeed, the very diversity of southern
women's lives makes it almost as perilous to generalize about *the*
southern woman as about *the* southerner. Despite such interpretive
disagreements, however, recent historians have agreed that southern
women's experiences were in many ways different from those of men,
and that attention to women therefore dictates a fundamental reconceptualization of important developments in southern history; as
Laura F. Edwards put it, "the inclusion of women in the history of
the nineteenth-century South changes our understanding of the Civil
War and Reconstruction."[16]

Such reconceptualization is evident over a wide range of topics in
nineteenth-century southern history, from life (both elite and en-

16. Elizabeth Fox-Genovese, *Within the Plantation Household: Black and White
Women of the Old South* (Chapel Hill: University of North Carolina Press, 1988); Suzanne
Lebsock, *The Free Women of Petersburg: Status and Culture in a Southern Town, 1784–1860*
(New York: W. W. Norton, 1984); Elizabeth R. Varon, *We Mean to Be Counted: White
Women and Politics in Antebellum Virginia* (Chapel Hill: University of North Carolina
Press, 1998); Laura F. Edwards, *Scarlett Doesn't Live Here Anymore: Southern Women in
the Civil War Era* (Urbana: University of Illinois Press, 2000), 2.

slaved) under the Peculiar Institution, the Civil War, and Reconstruction to the ways in which women participated in public affairs
and helped shape a supposedly all-male political process.[17] (Consider, as a simple example, the extent to which the debate over slave
"character" precipitated by Stanley M. Elkins was in fact a debate

17. For a sample of the rapidly burgeoning literature on white and black women in
slavery, war, and Reconstruction, see Anne Firor Scott, *The Southern Lady: From Pedestal
to Politics, 1830–1930* (Chicago: University of Chicago Press, 1970); Catherine Clinton, *The
Plantation Mistress: Woman's World in the Old South* (New York: Pantheon Books, 1982);
Fox-Genovese, *Within the Plantation Household*; Marli Frances Weiner, *Mistresses and
Slaves: Plantation Women in South Carolina, 1830–1880* (Urbana: University of Illinois
Press, 1997); Deborah Gray White, *Ar'n't I a Woman? Female Slaves in the Plantation
South* (New York: W. W. Norton, 1985); Jacqueline Jones, *Labor of Love, Labor of Sorrow:
Black Women, Work, and the Family from Slavery to the Present* (New York: Basic Books,
1985); Brenda E. Stevenson, *Life in Black and White: Family and Community in the Slave
South* (New York: Oxford University Press, 1996); Patricia Morton, ed., *Discovering the
Women in Slavery: Emancipating Perspectives on the American Past* (Athens: University
of Georgia Press, 1996); Stephanie M. H. Camp, "The Pleasures of Resistance: Enslaved
Women and Body Politics in the Plantation South, 1830–1861," *Journal of Southern His-
tory* 68 (August 2002): 533–72; Susana Delfino and Michele Gillespie, eds., *Neither Lady
nor Slave: Working Women of the Old South* (Chapel Hill: University of North Carolina
Press, 2002); George C. Rable, *Civil Wars: Women and the Crisis of Southern Nationalism*
(Urbana: University of Illinois Press, 1989); Drew Gilpin Faust, *Mothers of Invention:
Women of the Slaveholding South in the American Civil War* (Chapel Hill: University of
North Carolina Press, 1996); Leslie A. Schwalm, *A Hard Fight for We: Women's Transi-
tion from Slavery to Freedom in South Carolina* (Urbana: University of Illinois Press,
1997); Tera W. Hunter, *To 'Joy My Freedom: Southern Black Women's Lives and Labors
After the Civil War* (Cambridge, Mass.: Harvard University Press, 1997); and Noralee
Frankel, *Freedom's Women: Black Women and Families in Civil War Era Mississippi*
(Bloomington: Indiana University Press, 1999).

Work has been especially pronounced on women's political activities in the post-Reconstruction South. See Glenda Elizabeth Gilmore, *Gender and Jim Crow: Women and
the Politics of White Supremacy in North Carolina, 1896–1920* (Chapel Hill: University of
North Carolina Press, 1996); Anastatia Sims, *The Power of Femininity in the New South:
Women's Organizations and Politics in North Carolina, 1880–1930* (Columbia: University
of South Carolina Press, 1996); Elizabeth Hayes Turner, *Women, Culture, and Community: Religion and Reform in Galveston, 1880–1920* (New York: Oxford University Press,
1997); Judith N. McArthur, *Creating the New Woman: The Rise of Southern Women's Pro-
gressive Culture in Texas, 1893–1918* (Urbana: University of Illinois Press, 1998); and Elna
C. Green, *Southern Strategies: Southern Women and the Woman Suffrage Question*
(Chapel Hill: University of North Carolina Press, 1997). On earlier political efforts, see
Cynthia A. Kierner, *Beyond the Household: Women's Place in the Early South, 1700–1835*
(Ithaca, N.Y.: Cornell University Press, 1998); Victoria Bynum, *Unruly Women: The Poli-*

over the character of the *male* slave; *Sambo* was a male stereotype, and the debate over its legitimacy included discussion in liberal doses of such questions as whether "the" slave was really emasculated and whether *he* could protect *his* family.)[18] Meanwhile, a growing number of scholars have built upon insights in women's history to explore gender relations as both reflections and shapers of the social order in the nineteenth-century South. Paying attention to women and gender has been central to the historical revision that has reshaped our understanding of the South—and southerners—over the past generation.[19]

---

tics of Social and Sexual Control in the Old South (Chapel Hill: University of North Carolina Press, 1992); and Varon, *We Mean to Be Counted.*

18. "Although the merest hint of Sambo's 'manhood' might fill the Southern breast with scorn," wrote Elkins, "the child, 'in his place,' could be both exasperating and lovable." Elkins went on to emphasize the inability of the male slave to "protect the mother of his children except by appealing directly to the master." In his extended rebuttal of the Sambo thesis, John W. Blassingame also took for granted the male being of "the" slave: Blassingame conceded that "the slave faced almost insurmountable odds in his efforts to build a strong stable family. First and most important of all, his authority was restricted by his master. . . . The master, and not the slave, furnished the cabin, clothes, and the minimal food for his wife and children." In short, even as he challenged the Sambo thesis, Blassingame—unlike many historians writing in the 1980s and 1990s—did not challenge the way Elkins framed the debate; at the heart of the debate over "Sambo" was a debate over "the" slave's masculinity. Stanley M. Elkins, *Slavery: A Problem in American Institutional and Intellectual Life* (Chicago: University of Chicago Press, 1959), 82, 130; John W. Blassingame, *The Slave Community: Plantation Life in the Ante-Bellum South* (New York: Oxford University Press, 1972), 88.

19. Discussions of gender relations include Stephanie McCurry, *Masters of Small Worlds: Yeoman Households, Gender Relations, and the Political Culture of the Antebellum South Carolina Low Country* (New York: Oxford University Press, 1995); Joan E. Cashin, *A Family Venture: Men and Women on the Southern Frontier* (New York: Oxford University Press, 1991); LeeAnn Whites, *The Civil War as a Crisis in Gender: Augusta, Georgia, 1860–1890* (Athens: University of Georgia Press, 1995); Peter Bardaglio, *Reconstructing the Household: Families, Sex, and the Law in the Nineteenth-Century South* (Chapel Hill: University of North Carolina Press, 1995); Laura F. Edwards, *Gendered Strife and Confusion: The Political Culture of Reconstruction* (Urbana: University of Illinois Press, 1997); Amy Dru Stanley, *From Bondage to Contract: Wage Labor, Marriage, and the Market in the Age of Slave Emancipation* (Cambridge, Eng.: Cambridge University Press, 1998); Martha Hodes, *White Women, Black Men: Illicit Sex in the Nineteenth-Century South* (New Haven: Yale University Press, 1997); and Catherine Clinton and Nina Silber, eds., *Divided Houses: Gender and the Civil War* (New York: Oxford University Press, 1992).

Another important, but less studied, form of group variation is that occasioned by age. Despite the avalanche of writings on the Civil War, until James Marten's recent book virtually nothing had been written on the wartime experiences of a group that constituted more than one-third the population: children. There is reason to believe that age was an especially salient characteristic in nineteenth-century America, inhabited by a youthful population living in a self-consciously young nation, yet with some conspicuous exceptions age has been notably absent as an analytical category in historical interpretations of the era. In one of these exceptions, which provides a tantalizing glimpse of the extent to which age could divide nineteenth-century southerners, William Barney showed that in Alabama and Mississippi in 1860 and 1861, secessionist sentiment was disproportionately strong among young men: "[e]conomic status or occupation did not influence party affiliations so much as did age and social position," he argued, with Breckinridge Democrats preeminently representing "young slaveholders, lawyers, men on their way up driving for planter status."[20]

Historians have paid somewhat more attention to variation by

For works that synthesize and discuss recent research on women and gender in the nineteenth-century South, see Edwards, *Scarlett Doesn't Live Here Anymore*; Jacqueline Dowd Hall and Anne Firor Scott, "Women in the South," in *Interpreting Southern History: Historiographical Essays in Honor of Sanford W. Higginbotham,* ed. John B. Boles (Baton Rouge: Louisiana State University Press, 1987), 454–509; Drew Gilpin Faust, " 'Ours as Well as That of the Men': Women and Gender in the Civil War," in McPherson and Cooper, eds., *Writing the Civil War,* 228–40, 325–35; and J. William Harris, "Gender in the Recent History of the U.S. South and Some Speculations on the Prospects for Comparative History," in *The American South and the Italian Mezzogiorno: Essays in Comparative History,* ed. Enrico Dal Lago and Rick Halpern (Houndsmill, Eng.: Palgrave, 2002), 155–72.

20. James Marten, *The Children's Civil War* (Chapel Hill: University of North Carolina Press, 1998); William L. Barney, *The Secessionist Impulse: Alabama and Mississippi in 1860* (Princeton: Princeton University Press, 1974), 50–100 (quotations: 100). For an analysis of "Young America" as a manifestation of a self-conscious youthful exuberance in the antebellum era, see George B. Forgie, *Patricide in the House Divided: A Psychological Interpretation of Lincoln and His Age* (New York: W. W. Norton, 1979), esp. 89–122. Although he did not focus on the South, Forgie offered an imaginative application of generational-cohort analysis to explore tensions besetting Americans in the "post-heroic" era of the 1830s–1850s.

age under slavery. Studies of slave occupations have noted the extent to which these occupations were age- (as well as gender-) specific: children formed a high proportion of house servants, for example, and elderly slaves no longer fit for strenuous labor often received "lighter" assignments that could range from gardening to child-care. The long-neglected story of children in slavery has finally begun to receive the attention it deserves in books by Wilma King and Marie Jenkins Schwartz. At the most basic level, this story is important because at any given point in time approximately half—in some areas well over half—of all slaves were children. Their lives displayed contradictory characteristics, suggesting that in some ways their lot was less oppressive than that of their elders but that in other ways it was even worse. If many young slaves were barely aware of their unfree status—"the first seven or eight years of the slave boy's life," recalled Frederick Douglass, "are about as full of sweet content as those of the most favored and petted *white* children of the slave-holder"—recent research also reveals that far more than adults, slave children typically received insufficient food rations, which seriously retarded their physical growth. Clearly, the lives of children in slavery were in a variety of ways different from those of adults, and histories that ignore children must be as partial as those that ignore women. But the experiences of young slaves is doubly significant because so much of our understanding of antebellum slavery rests on the recollections of those who knew slavery only as children; of the slaves interviewed for the Federal Writers' Project, about two-thirds had been under ten years old at the start of the Civil War and the vast majority had been under twenty.[21]

21. Wilma King, *Stolen Childhood: Slave Youth in Nineteenth-Century America* (Bloomington: Indiana University Press, 1995); Marie Jenkins Schwartz, *Born in Bondage: Growing Up Enslaved in the Antebellum South* (Cambridge, Mass.: Harvard University Press, 2000); Frederick Douglass, *My Bondage and My Freedom* (1855; New York: Dover, 1969), 40. On the insufficient diet of slave children, see Robert William Fogel, *Without Consent or Contract: The Rise and Fall of American Slavery* (New York: W. W. Norton, 1989), 142–44; on the life-cycle of slave occupations, see ibid., 52–58. On the age of ex-slaves interviewed for the Federal Writers' Project, see Paul D. Escott, *Slavery Remembered: A Record of Twentieth-Century Slave Narratives* (Chapel Hill: University of North Carolina Press, 1979), 16–17.

—⁓—

Because the Confederate rebellion constituted an attempt to form a southern "nation," the behavior and beliefs of southerners during the Civil War are especially pertinent to efforts to explore southern unity and disunity. From the beginning, two competing myths surfaced, one proclaiming the solidarity of the entire southern "people" in the wake of Yankee aggression and the other portraying the Confederacy as the product of a conspiracy foisted on "loyal" southerners by either selfish aristocrats or power-hungry traitors—in the words of Tennessee's firebrand Unionist agitator Parson Brownlow, men who, "for the purpose of hiding their traitorous course, create a false issue before the people." If these myths first emerged in the propaganda efforts of Civil War protagonists, they found ready support after the war among those eager to justify their wartime behavior and among subsequent generations seeking to salvage from the Civil War carnage a meaningful legacy of heroism and purpose. The struggle over the war's meaning was just beginning in 1865.[22]

Although the starkest versions of these competing stereotypes no longer find much support among historians, scholars continue to disagree sharply over the degree of southern support for the Confederacy, the nature of Confederate nationalism, and the viability of the Confederacy as a "nation." Some, such as the authors of a book entitled *Why the South Lost the Civil War,* have seen insufficient nationalism as a cause of Confederate defeat. "The Confederates lacked a feeling of oneness, that almost mystical sense of nationhood," they declared. "The Confederate nation was created on

22. For a recent book puncturing the myth of self-sacrificing Confederate "ladies," see Faust, *Mothers of Invention,* esp. 234–47. For the wartime writings of Brownlow, see Stephen V. Ash, ed., *Secessionists and Other Scoundrels: Selections from Parson Brownlow's Book* (Baton Rouge: Louisiana State University Press, 1999), 65 (quotation). For other examples of southern Unionists blaming secession on slaveholding aristocrats, see Jon L. Wakelyn, ed., *Southern Unionist Pamphlets and the Civil War* (Columbia: University of Missouri Press, 1999). On postwar southern mythmaking, see Gaines M. Foster, *Ghosts of the Confederacy: Defeat, the Lost Cause, and the Emergence of the New South* (New York: Oxford University Press, 1987); Kirk Savage, *Standing Soldiers, Kneeling Slaves: Race, War, and Monument in Nineteenth-Century America* (Princeton: Princeton University Press, 1997); and David W. Blight, *Race and Reunion: The Civil War in American Memory* (Cambridge, Mass.: Harvard University Press, 2001).

paper, not in the hearts and minds of its would-be citizens." Others, such as James McPherson and Drew Gilpin Faust, have cautioned against working backward from the ultimate Confederate defeat to argue that this defeat was in some sense preordained. In her insightful book *The Creation of Confederate Nationalism,* Faust warned that nationalism was "not a substance available to a people in a certain premeasured amount" so much as a "dynamic of ideas and social realities" that needed to be *created*; "comparative history reminds us," she noted, "that nationalism is more often than not 'insufficient' at the time of its first expression." In another work, however, Faust suggested that lack of support among white women was fatal to the Confederacy; tackling head-on one of the most passionately held and enduring myths associated with the Confederacy—that of the selfless loyalty of its women—she concluded that "it may well be because of its women that the South lost the Civil War."[23]

The most recent case for southern wartime unity has been made by Gary W. Gallagher in his book *The Confederate War.* Complaining that "historians employing the analytical prism of class, gender, and race have focused almost exclusively on sources of division," he countered that far from collapsing as a result of internal weaknesses, the Confederacy survived for so long because it aroused an extraordinary level of popular support, even under brutally adverse conditions. Noting that more than three-quarters of the South's white men of military age served in the Confederate military, Gallagher stressed the patriotic devotion of white southerners—male and female—to the Confederate cause. "Confederates by the thousands from all classes exhibited a strong identification with their country,"

23. Richard E. Beringer et al., *Why the South Lost the Civil War* (Athens: University of Georgia Press, 1986), 64 (quotation); James M. McPherson, "Why Did the Confederacy Lose?" (1992), reprinted in McPherson, *Drawn with the Sword: Reflections on the American Civil War* (New York: Oxford University Press, 1996), 113–36; Drew Gilpin Faust, *The Creation of Confederate Nationalism: Ideology and Identity in the Civil War South* (Baton Rouge: Louisiana State University Press, 1988), 6 (quotation), and "Altars of Sacrifice: Confederate Women and the Narratives of War," in her *Southern Stories: Slaveholders in Peace and War* (Columbia: University of Missouri Press, 1992), 113–40 (quotation: 140).

he concluded, "and ended the war still firmly committed to the idea of an independent southern nation."[24]

Gallagher's case is a strong one—within narrow confines. Clearly, millions of southern whites believed passionately in the Confederate cause, and many continued for decades after the war to be consumed by bitter hatred of their Yankee conquerors. But the intensity of such feelings among many southerners cannot negate their absence among others and does not speak to the question of southern unity or disunity. Nor can Gallagher's sources—more than three hundred letters from enthusiastic supporters of the Confederacy—establish southern unity, especially given that few of these letters are from yeoman farmers or poor whites and none are from blacks. Indeed, in *The South Versus the South*, William W. Freehling has issued a direct challenge to Gallagher's thesis, emphasizing the many white and black southerners who *opposed* the Confederate rebellion and helped bring about its defeat; pointing out that "white Confederates were only half the Southerners," he concluded that "the divided southern home front crippled Confederate battlefield heroes."[25]

24. Gary W. Gallagher, *The Confederate War* (Cambridge, Mass.: Harvard University Press, 1997), 27, 71 (quotations), 28 (statistic). For a similar argument based on a statewide study, see William Blair, *Virginia's Private War: Feeding Body and Soul in the Confederacy, 1861–1865* (New York: Oxford University Press, 1998).

25. William W. Freehling, *The South Versus the South* (New York: Oxford University Press, 2001), xii. For evidence of disunity among southern whites *during* the war, see, among others, Stephen Ambrose, "Yeoman Discontent in the Confederacy," *Civil War History* 8 (1962): 259–68; Paul D. Escott, *After Secession: Jefferson Davis and the Failure of Confederate Nationalism* (Baton Rouge: Louisiana State University Press, 1978); William W. Freehling, "The Divided South, the Causes of Confederate Defeat, and the Reintegration of Narrative History," in his *The Reintegration of American History: Slavery and the Civil War* (New York: Oxford University Press, 1994), 220–52; David Williams, *Rich Man's War: Class, Caste, and Confederate Defeat in the Lower Chattahoochie Valley* (Athens: University of Georgia Press, 1998); Thomas G. Dyer, *Secret Yankees: The Union Circle in Confederate Atlanta* (Baltimore: Johns Hopkins University Press, 1999); Daniel E. Sutherland, ed., *Guerrillas, Unionists, and Violence on the Confederate Home Front* (Fayetteville: University of Arkansas Press, 1999); Mark E. Neely Jr., *Southern Rights: Political Prisoners and the Myth of Confederate Constitutionalism* (Charlottesville: University Press of Virginia, 1999), 99–150; Mark A. Weitz, *A Higher Duty: Desertion Among Georgia Troops During the Civil War* (Lincoln: University of Nebraska Press, 2000); John C. Inscoe and Gordon B. McKinney, *The Heart of Confederate Appalachia: Western North Carolina in the Civil War* (Chapel Hill: University of North Carolina Press, 2000); John C. Inscoe and Robert C. Kenzer, eds., *Enemies of the Country: New Perspectives on*

I shall return in chapter 3 to the question of creating southern nationalism, a question that I think is best approached in comparison with similar efforts elsewhere, but it is worth noting now that the degree of southern support one finds for the Confederacy depends in great measure on how one defines both *southern* and *support*. Freehling agreed with Gallagher that "the vast majority of Confederate state whites long supported their new nation," but added the important qualification that "the vast majority of other Southerners either opposed the rebel cause or cared not whether it lived or died." Although this judgment depended in part on defining as southerners the residents of the four border slave states that remained in the Union, a definition not everyone is likely to accept, it also in some ways overstated white unity *within* the Confederacy by minimizing the extent to which sentiment changed over time: indeed, if the great majority of white southerners can be described as identifying strongly with the Confederacy at some point in time, many of those same southerners expressed serious reservations either earlier or later. More important, counting all southerners, black as well as white, it is likely that in no state with the possible exception of Texas did secession ever represent the will of the majority.[26]

Unionists in the Civil War South (Athens: University of Georgia Press, 2001); and Victoria E. Bynum, *The Free State of Jones: Mississippi's Longest Civil War* (Chapel Hill: University of North Carolina Press, 2001). On *pro*-Confederate dissent in an area dominated by Unionists, see W. Todd Groce, *Mountain Rebels: East Tennessee Confederates and the Civil War, 1860–1870* (Knoxville: University of Tennessee Press, 1999).

26. Freehling, *The South Versus the South*, xii. My calculation of the absence of a prosecession majority is based on the propositions that (1) support for secession among blacks was minimal, and (2) support for secession among whites ranged from overwhelming in many plantation districts of the Deep South to a minority position in most of Appalachia. For the more extreme judgment that "at no time during the winter of 1860–1861 was secession desired by a majority of the [*white*] people of the slave states," see David M. Potter, *Lincoln and His Party in the Secession Crisis* (New Haven: Yale University Press, 1942), 208. Important works on the secession of southern states include Steven A. Channing, *Crisis of Fear: Secession in South Carolina* (New York: Simon and Schuster, 1970); Barney, *The Secessionist Impulse*; Michael P. Johnson, *Toward a Patriarchal Republic: The Secession of Georgia* (Baton Rouge: Louisiana State University Press, 1977); Daniel W. Crofts, *Reluctant Confederates: Upper South Unionists in the Secession Crisis* (Chapel Hill: University of North Carolina Press, 1989); and Peyton McCrary, Clark Miller, and Dale Baum, "Class and Party in the Secession Crisis: Voting Behavior in the Deep

In this context, I think that it is important to emphasize that the term *southerner* encompasses blacks as well as whites. In 1860, one-third of all southerners were slaves, yet in the conventional terminology of both contemporaries and historians, to be proslavery was to be "prosouthern" and to be antislavery was to be "antisouthern." Clearly, however, this terminology—although widely used—is ideologically laden. If it was second nature for contemporaries to describe abolitionists as antisouthern, there is no reason for *us* to accept such usage (although historians frequently do so): after all, from the point of view of many southerners, the abolitionists were *pro*southern—as were the proponents of a radical Reconstruction policy in the 1860s or a sweeping civil rights program in the 1960s. Use of the conventional terminology pre-defines the South as conservative, racist, and unchanging—something that *one* South was but that others were not.[27]

The existence of many Souths is especially evident in the post–Civil War era, when the shift from slavery to free labor and from Confederate to American nationality generated strikingly diverse versions of southern identity. One important form of postwar southern diversity can be seen in the geographic variability of Reconstruction. In

---

South," *Journal of Interdisciplinary History* 8 (1978): 429–57. For a challenge to the idea that antebellum Richmonders identified monolithically as southerners, and a suggestion of shallow support for the Confederacy, see Gregg D. Kimball, *American City, Southern Place: A Cultural History of Antebellum Richmond* (Athens: University of Georgia Press, 2000). Of the seven Deep South states that seceded before the firing on Fort Sumter, Texas had by far the smallest concentration of African Americans—about 30 percent of its population. (In each of the other six, blacks formed at least 44 percent of the population.) On secession politics in Texas, see Dale Baum, *The Shattering of Texas Unionism: Politics in the Lone Star State During the Civil War Era* (Baton Rouge: Louisiana State University Press, 1998), esp. 42–81. On wartime Unionism in Texas, see David Pickering and Judy Falls, *Brush Men and Vigilantes: Civil War Dissent in Texas* (College Station: Texas A&M Press, 2000).

27. James C. Cobb has noted the "strong and apparently still strengthening inclination of blacks in the South to identify as southerners" in the "post–Civil Rights era"; one might suggest that this inclination was equally as notable during the first as during the second Reconstruction. Cobb, "Searching for Southernness: Community and Identity in the Contemporary South," in Cobb, *Redefining Southern Culture: Mind and Identity in the Modern South* (Athens: University of Georgia Press, 1999), 127.

some states, such as Louisiana, Florida, South Carolina, and Mississippi, Republican governments remained in power for about a decade, whereas in others, including Tennessee, North Carolina, Virginia, and Georgia, they lasted only two or three years before the process of "redemption" ushered in "home rule" and an end to Reconstruction. Reconstruction also produced far more radical changes in some states than in others: to take one simple index, whereas at least 226 African Americans from Mississippi and 314 from South Carolina held public office between 1867 and 1877, only 46 blacks from Arkansas and 20 from Tennessee served in such positions. South Carolina and Mississippi sent 8 African Americans to the United States Congress, including two senators and six representatives; Arkansas and Tennessee sent none. And within individual states there were similar divisions with respect to both the persistence of Republican rule and the frequency with which blacks exercised political power.[28]

When these variations in Reconstruction experience are examined in the context of *southern* characteristics, it becomes clear that the most southern states—as defined in chapter 1 in terms of the prevalence of slavery and enthusiasm for secession—were also the states that underwent the most intense Reconstruction experiences. The three Confederate states with the shortest reconstructions—Tennessee, North Carolina, and Virginia—were all Upper South states that seceded only after the firing on Fort Sumter; in each of these states, slaves had constituted under 35 percent of the population in 1860. By contrast, the four states with the longest reconstructions—Louisiana, Florida, Mississippi, and South Carolina—were all Deep South states that seceded before the firing on Fort Sumter; in each of these states, slaves had made up more than 40 percent of the population. What is more, the border states experienced what can be termed "border reconstructions": if as loyal states that had re-

---

28. Foner, *Reconstruction,* passim, esp. 346–459, 564–601; Peter Kolchin, "Scalawags, Carpetbaggers, and Reconstruction: A Quantitative Look at Southern Congressional Politics, 1868–1872," *Journal of Southern History* 45 (February 1979): 63–76. On black officeholding, see Eric Foner, *Freedom's Lawmakers: A Directory of Black Officeholders During Reconstruction* (New York: Oxford University Press, 1993), statistics: xiv.

mained in the Union they were not subject to Congressional Reconstruction, they nevertheless grappled with many of the same postwar problems that the former Confederate states did, including most notably the construction of free-labor societies in the wake of slavery's demise, and they saw the rise of such key Reconstruction institutions as the Republican Party, the Freedmen's Bureau, and public schools. Indeed, with these variations in mind, one could easily stand a traditional assumption on its head by suggesting that *support* for Reconstruction provides a useful index of southernness in the years after the Civil War.[29]

As this assertion suggests, southerners were by no means of one mind in the post–Civil War years; rather than speaking of the "mind" of the South, one must explore the "minds" of the South. In recognizing this diversity, historians have put forth differing versions of the multiple southern identities that existed in the last third of the nineteenth century. C. Vann Woodward, for example, delineated "three alternative philosophies of race relations" that struggled for ascendance among white southerners in the era of "forgotten alternatives" after the end of Reconstruction: a "conservative" philosophy of "paternalism and *noblesse oblige*," a "radical" philosophy based on defense of common folks' class interests, and a less-widespread but forcefully articulated "liberal" philosophy that embraced equal rights for blacks and whites. "All three of these alternative philosophies rejected the doctrines of extreme racism," Woodward noted, "and all three were indigenously and thoroughly Southern in origin." Joel Williamson used the same terminology as Woodward to describe different kinds of white southerners: *his* "Liberals" were racial agnostics who "did not yet know the potential of the Negro," his "Conservatives" sought to keep blacks in their place with a mini-

---

29. The duration of Reconstruction governments is drawn from David Herbert Donald, Jean H. Baker, and Michael F. Holt, *The Civil War and Reconstruction* (New York: W. W. Norton, 2001), 574; statistics on slavery are from Kolchin, *American Slavery,* 242. On Reconstruction in the border states, see Richard O. Curry, ed., *Radicalism, Racism, and Party Realignment: The Border States During Reconstruction* (Baltimore: Johns Hopkins Press, 1969). On the post-emancipation construction of a free-labor society in Maryland, see Richard Paul Fuke, *Imperfect Equality: African Americans and the Confines of White Racial Attitudes in Post-Emancipation Maryland* (New York: Fordham University Press, 1999).

mum of fuss, and his "Radicals" were pathological extremists who "insisted that there was *no place* for the Negro in the future of American society, and, moreover, that his disappearance was imminent." But if he differed from Woodward in evaluating the specific characteristics of white racial thought in the late nineteenth century, Williamson agreed with him in rejecting the notion of a solid South; both depicted a continuing struggle over the nature of the South among what were, in effect, *different* Souths. And we must remember that in doing so, they focused on only *part* of southern diversity; *black* southerners had their own (also far from united) visions of what it meant to be southern. "To scratch the surface of the 'solid South' in the late nineteenth century," Jane Dailey has noted in her compelling exploration of the Readjuster movement in post-Reconstruction Virginia, "was to discover multiple competing interest groups divided by region, race, ideology, and class."[30]

Recently, historians have devoted considerable attention to the struggle over the meaning of emancipation—that is, what the shift from a slave South and a Confederate South to a free-labor American South would mean to those who lived below the Mason-Dixon Line. Because the old social order was overthrown but the nature of the new was as yet unclear, the post-emancipation period was a time of great fluidity in which the very nature of the South—and what it meant to be "southern"—was up for grabs. Among the plethora of competing visions, historians have delineated three broad ideological positions, each reflecting a particular interest, that vied for ascendancy. The shape of the New South was forged in the crucible of this bitter struggle.[31]

30. Woodward, *The Strange Career of Jim Crow*, 3^d rev. ed. (New York: Oxford University Press, 1974), 31–65 (quotations: 44, 49, 45); Joel Williamson, *The Crucible of Race: Black-White Relations in the American South Since Emancipation* (New York: Oxford University Press, 1984), 4–7, 79–323 (quotations: 5, 6); Jane Dailey, *Before Jim Crow: The Politics of Race in Postemancipation Virginia* (Chapel Hill: University of North Carolina Press, 2000), 4. See also Michael R. Hyman, *The Anti-Redeemers: Hill-Country Political Dissenters in the Lower South from Redemption to Populism* (Baton Rouge: Louisiana State University Press, 1990).

31. Among the many historians who have explored the post-emancipation South, Eric Foner has most clearly set forth the nature of this three-way struggle. See *Reconstruction*, 77–175, and especially "Reconstruction and the Crisis of Free Labor," in his *Politics and Ideology in the Age of the Civil War* (New York: Oxford University Press, 1980), 97–127.

Most former slaves strove above all else to maximize their autonomy, to get as far as possible from slavelike dependence. They vigorously defended the integrity of their families, resisting with
particular tenacity widespread efforts of whites to retain control of
young blacks by having them "apprenticed" to their former owners.
They quickly seceded from southern white churches, as the once-
"invisible church" came out into the open and assumed a prominent
place in black communities. They struggled to secure the most independent form of labor relations, seeking to acquire their own land
but when that proved impossible—as it usually did—often express-
ing a preference for sharecropping over wage labor because the
cropper seemed more independent than the wage laborer, less under
the control of white authorities in ways that reminded them of slavery. But most of all, as people whose lives had been under constant
supervision, they sought to do things their own way, without having
to beg for permission. Shortly after the war, when northern reporter
Whitelaw Reid found a black man squatting in an abandoned tent
outside Selma and questioned him about his intentions, the reply
was telling: "I's want to be a free man, cum when I please, and no-
body say nuffin' to me, nor order me roun'."[32]

Former slaveowners, by contrast, typically strove to maintain as
many of their old prerogatives as possible—in the process *limiting*
the autonomy of their former slaves—as they tried to make sense of
a bewildering and frightening new world. As James L. Roark has

32. The quotation is from Whitelaw Reid, *After the War: A Tour of the Southern
States, 1865–1866,* ed. C. Vann Woodward (1866; New York: Harper & Row, 1965), 389. In
recent decades, historians have devoted considerable attention to the postwar struggle of
African Americans for autonomy; for my early version of this story, see Peter Kolchin,
First Freedom: The Responses of Alabama's Blacks to Emancipation and Reconstruction
(Westport, Conn.: Greenwood Press, 1972). For two of many recent state studies, see
Julie Saville, *The Work of Reconstruction: From Slave to Wage Laborer in South Carolina,
1860–1870* (New York: Cambridge University Press, 1994); and Lynda J. Morgan, *Emanci-
pation in Virginia's Tobacco Belt, 1850–1870* (Athens: University of Georgia Press, 1992).
For an interesting examination of household economy among freedpeople in Granville
County, North Carolina, see Sharon Ann Holt, *Making Freedom Pay: North Carolina
Freedpeople Working for Themselves, 1865–1900* (Athens: University of Georgia Press, 2000).
The whole South is covered in Leon F. Litwack, *Been in the Storm So Long: The After-
math of Slavery* (New York: Alfred A. Knopf, 1979).

shown in his perceptive volume *Masters Without Slaves,* southern planters found the postwar South a bewildering new world. "Almost overnight," he wrote, "Southern planters crossed from the world of slave labor to that of compensated labor, from substantial wealth and ease to relative poverty and drudgery, from political dominance to crippled influence. . . . From the planters' perspective, the postbellum plantation was almost unrecognizable." Accustomed to directing subservient labor, the former masters sought desperately to maintain as much as possible of their old authority and of labor's dependence, even trying unsuccessfully to lure immigrant laborers to toil in their fields when black workers proved too insistent on their rights. Accepting the legal abolition of slavery, most white landowners strove nevertheless to minimize abolition's consequences and keep the postbellum South as much like the antebellum South as possible. In the process, they unwittingly fostered significant change, as men who had once boasted of the paternalistic care they showed for their "people" now relied "upon the coercions of the market place to motivate black labor" and sought to distance themselves from their "ungrateful" charges. An intense class struggle dominated the countryside in the Reconstruction South.[33]

Between the irreconcilable goals of the former slaves and former masters, there was a third vision for the post-emancipation South, one articulated most forcefully by agents of the Freedmen's Bureau and other spokesmen for newly triumphant "free-labor" ideals but also embraced by a substantial number of white southerners (some former slaveowners and some persons of more modest means) who now welcomed the abolition of chattel slavery as the precondition for a new, modernizing South. This vision fully satisfied neither most planters nor most freedpeople. On the one hand, it presupposed "fair" compensation and civil rights for former slaves; on the other, it preached the virtues not of black autonomy and landownership but those of discipline, contract, and wage labor. Insisting that white employers treat their black employees like free men and women, free-labor ideologues urged those employees to be orderly,

---

33. James L. Roark, *Masters Without Slaves: Southern Planters in the Civil War and Reconstruction* (New York: W. W. Norton, 1977), quotations: 196, 144.

hardworking, and cheerful. Less than a month after the war's end, for example, Brigadier General C. C. Andrews issued a proclamation "To the Freedmen of Selma and Vicinity" instructing them on their new responsibilities: "It will greatly rejoice the hearts of your friends all over the world if you show that you are worthy of freedom," he intoned. "Be industrious, be charitable and kind in your feelings; be peaceable, forbearing, sober; cherish no spite." Suggesting that "good behavior" was the key to earning public respect, he explained that "liberty alone is not happiness. Self-control and self-support are required to make it pleasant." In short, in propounding the bourgeois virtues of work, order, discipline, sobriety, diligence, and honesty, free-labor spokesmen emphasized what Bureau Commissioner O. O. Howard termed the "duties as well as privileges of freedom."[34]

If freedpeople, planters, and free-labor spokesmen articulated three broadly differing visions of the post-emancipation South, each of these in turn encompassed a variety of overlapping and competing positions. Southern blacks expressed diverse aspirations and took advantage of new opportunities in differing ways. Some eagerly embraced participation in the commercial economy whereas others—especially in the lowcountry of South Carolina and Georgia—showed a preference for cultivating food crops rather than staples that in its most extreme form fostered a condition approaching quasi-peasant autarky. Some, especially in cities, sought to promote the nineteenth-century version of integration known as "social equality," but many, especially in rural areas of the Deep South, took advantage of their new mobility to associate *less* rather than more with whites; this growing separation was manifested in diverse ways, including the widespread secession of blacks from white-controlled churches, the emergence of labor relations such as sharecropping that entailed less physical supervision by white authorities, and

34. Quotations are from C. C. Andrews, "To the Freedmen of Selma and Vicinity," 9 May 1865, in *The War of the Rebellion: A Compilation of the Official Records of the Union and Confederate Armies,* Ser. I, Vol. XLIX, part 2 (Washington: Government Printing Office, 1897), 729; and O. O. Howard speech, quoted in Stanley, *From Bondage to Contract,* 36.

migration patterns that—at least in much of the Deep South—made black-dominated areas blacker and white-dominated areas whiter.[35]

African Americans differed in their political views as well. Although the vast majority enthusiastically supported the Republican Party—the party of freedom—they expressed different goals and followed differing strategies for achieving those goals. Contrast, for example, the moderate tone of the Alabama Colored Convention of November 1865, whose resolution emphasized the need for blacks to "work industriously and honestly" and to pursue "peace, friendship, and good will toward all men—especially toward our white fellow-citizens among whom our lot is cast," with the radicalism of firebrands such as Tunis Campbell and Aaron Bradley, whose militant agitation for equal rights and land-distribution in lowcountry Georgia sent shivers down the spines of respectable society. In general, blacks became increasingly assertive in politics as Reconstruction progressed—at least in the states where they continued to have political rights—insisting that in constituting the great majority of Republican voters, they also deserved a significant role in the party's leadership. As a result, even as Republican control of the South eroded, Republican-controlled states elected an increasing number of black government officials; the number of African American congressmen, for example, increased from three in the 41st Congress (1869–71) to five in the 42nd (1871–73) and seven in both the 43rd (1873–75) and 44th (1875–77). But even in their growing assertiveness they pursued diverse strategies, with some choosing to press their views on the Republicans by threatening—or in some cases going

35. Generalizations in this and the next five paragraphs are based on extensive reading in post-emancipation primary and secondary sources. On rejection of production for market and preference for cooperative landholding among lowcountry freedpeople, see Edward Magdol, *A Right to the Land: Essays on the Freedmen's Community* (Westport, Conn.: Greenwood Press, 1976); Eric Foner, *Nothing But Freedom: Emancipation and Its Legacy* (Baton Rouge: Louisiana State University Press, 1983), 74–110; and Saville, *The Work of Reconstruction*, esp. 42–70. On urban race relations, see Howard N. Rabinowitz, *Race Relations in the Urban South, 1865–1890* (New York: Oxford University Press, 1978); for migration leading to the growing physical separation of blacks and whites in rural Alabama, see Kolchin, *First Freedom,* 14–19. For an emphasis on the diversity of black (and white) responses to emancipation, see Litwack, *Been in the Storm So Long.*

further than threatening—to back independent or Democratic chal-
lengers, while most adhered loyally to the Grand Old Party.[36]

Planters, too, responded to changed conditions in diverse ways.
Some expressed their disgust with new conditions by absenting
themselves from their troublesome former property, becoming ab-
sentee owners whose only real concern with their plantations was
for the income they provided. The most extreme version of this separation resulted in the actual emigration of thousands of southerners, including several hundred who strove to recreate a slaveholder's
paradise in Brazil, but even when they remained physically present,
the shift from what Gavin Wright termed "laborlords to landlords"
inevitably resulted in reduced contact between planters and freedpeople. Planters who remained at home struggled in a variety of
ways to adjust to their radically changed relationship with their former slaves. Many—in some areas most, if one believes complaints
by freedpeople and reports of Freedmen's Bureau agents—found it
impossible to accept the notion of dealing with their former property as free people and resorted to various tactics to cheat them out
of their earnings, including finding pretexts to expel sharecroppers
from their plantations after most of the season's labor was done but
before the crop was divided; as a result of such deceptive practices,
Mississippi Bureau Assistant Commissioner Alvan C. Gillem noted
the "strange fact" in early 1867 "that those freedmen who worked
on shares during the past year insist upon stipulated wages, while
those who worked for wages are anxious to work for shares." Some

36. The quotation from the Alabama Colored Convention is from the *New York
Daily Tribune*, 12 December 1865. On Campbell and Bradley, see Russell Duncan, *Freedom's Shore: Tunis Campbell and the Georgia Freedmen* (Athens: University of Georgia
Press, 1986); and Joseph P. Reidy, "Aaron A. Bradley: Voice of Black Labor in the Georgia Lowcountry," in *Southern Black Leaders of the Reconstruction Era*, ed. Howard N.
Rabinowitz (Urbana: University of Illinois Press, 1982), 281–308. On political divisions
among blacks in one southern city, see Michael W. Fitzgerald, *Urban Emancipation: Politics in Reconstruction Mobile, 1860–1890* (Baton Rouge: Louisiana State University Press,
2002). On the general subject of southern blacks in Reconstruction politics, see Foner,
Reconstruction, esp. 110–19, 281–306, 316–33, 346–79, 535–63; Foner, *Freedom's Lawmakers*; Thomas Holt, *Black Over White: Political Leadership in South Carolina During Reconstruction* (Urbana: University of Illinois Press, 1977); and Rabinowitz, ed., *Southern
Black Leaders*.

planters enlisted the Ku Klux Klan and other terroristic organizations to keep their laborers in line and combat the new order; others, like Mississippi's James K. Alcorn, *accepted* the new order and became active in the Republican Party.[37]

Diversity also characterized the positions of the men in the middle, of whom I shall consider only two important groups. If Freedmen's Bureau officials were generally supporters of "free labor," they had widely varying views of what this meant and how it should be instituted. Some Bureau officials clearly saw the greatest threat to "free labor" coming from planters who failed to recognize that blacks were really free, whether this meant trying to cheat workers of their hard-earned wages or gain control over black families by arranging to have children forcibly apprenticed to whites, indeed often to former owners; across the South, agents echoed Alvan Gillem's concerns and took what steps they could to protect the freedpeople in their newly won rights. Other Bureau officials, however, were more concerned about the possibility that blacks would refuse to *labor* than that they would fail to be *free* and cooperated with planters in their efforts to secure a cheap, docile, and orderly labor force. Indeed, Superintendent Howard himself, a man of strong egalitarian impulses, observed that after the war the Bureau "came to the assistance of the Planters" and that one of its most noteworthy achievements was turning the former slaves into "reliable labor-

---

37. The quotation is from Alvan C. Gillem to Commissioner Howard, Vicksburg, Mississippi, 20 January 1867, letters received, Assistant Adjutant General's Office, Freedmen's Bureau Papers (National Archives); for Gillem's continuing discussion of planters' efforts to cheat laborers, see his reports of 15 July, 5 August, 13 August, 10 October, and 28 November, ibid. Gavin Wright's formulation of the shift from "laborlord to landlord" appears in his book *Old South, New South: Revolutions in the Southern Economy Since the Civil War* (New York: Basic Books, 1986), 17–50. On white violence and terrorism, see esp. Allen W. Trelease, *White Terror: The Ku Klux Klan Conspiracy and Southern Reconstruction* (New York: Harper & Row, 1971); George C. Rable, *But There Was No Peace: The Role of Violence in the Politics of Reconstruction* (Athens: University of Georgia Press, 1984); and Kenneth C. Barnes, *Who Killed John Clayton? Political Violence and the Emergence of the New South, 1861–1893* (Durham: Duke University Press, 1998). On Alcorn, see Lillian A. Pereyra, *James Lusk Alcorn: Persistent Whig* (Baton Rouge: Louisiana State University Press, 1966). The best study of the planters' varied responses to emancipation remains Roark, *Masters Without Slaves.*

ers under the free system." Sometimes, this effort to create "reliable laborers" entailed outright violence. "My predecessors here worked with a view to please the white citizens, at the expense of, and injustice to, the Freedmen," complained assistant superintendent A. Geddis in November 1865, after arriving at his new post in Tuskegee, Alabama. "They have invariably given permission to inflict punishment for insolence or idleness, and have detailed soldiers to tie up and otherwise punish the laborers who have, in the opinion of the employers, been *refractory*." No wonder a number of historians have concluded—inaccurately, I believe—that the Freedmen's Bureau as a whole operated essentially in support of planter interests; *some* Bureau agents did.[38]

White southerners who strove to come to terms with the new order—so-called "scalawags"—showed equal heterogeneity. For many years, scholars endeavored to create a composite portrait of the typical scalawag, with some describing him as a former Whig who continued to see the Democratic Party as the enemy and others countering with an upcountry yeoman who resented the hegemony of planter-aristocrats and saw the Republican Party as a tool to undermine that hegemony.[39] More recently, however, this debate has

38. Quotations are from Howard to Charles Nordhoff, Washington, 19 March 1866, letters sent, Assistant Adjutant General's Office, Freedmen's Bureau Papers; and A. Geddis to Assistant Commissioner Wager Swayne, Tuskegee, Alabama, 7 September 1865, Alabama Operations Report, Freedmen's Bureau Papers. For examples of works critical of the Freedmen's Bureau, see William S. McFeely, *Yankee Stepfather: General O. O. Howard and the Freedmen* (New Haven: Yale University Press, 1968); and Thomas J. May, "Continuity and Change in the Labor Program of the Union Army and Freedmen's Bureau," *Civil War History* 17 (September 1971): 245–54. Most recent judgments are more nuanced; see, for example, Paul A. Cimbala, *Under the Guardianship of the Nation: The Freedmen's Bureau and the Reconstruction of Georgia, 1865–1870* (Athens: University of Georgia Press, 1997); and Cimbala and Miller, eds., *The Freedmen's Bureau and Reconstruction*.

39. For the early debate, see David H. Donald, "The Scalawag in Mississippi Reconstruction," *Journal of Southern History* 10 (November 1944): 447–60; Thomas B. Alexander, "Persistent Whiggery in the Confederate South, 1860–1877," *Journal of Southern History* 27 (August 1961): 305–29; Allen W. Trelease, "Who Were the Scalawags?" *Journal of Southern History* 29 (November 1963): 445–68; Otto H. Olsen, "Reconsidering the Scalawags," *Civil War History* 12 (December 1966): 304–20; Warren A. Ellem, "Who Were the Mississippi Scalawags?" *Journal of Southern History* 38 (May 1972): 217–40; and

yielded to the recognition that *both* portraits are accurate, although incomplete. For one thing, the old debate tended to obscure the distinction between Republican *politicians,* many of whom did have Whiggish-planter backgrounds, and white Republican *voters,* the majority of whom hailed from upcountry regions with strong Unionist predilections. For another, it is clear that different kinds of white southerners became Republicans for different reasons. Some were blackbelt planters while others were upcountry yeomen, some were former Unionists while others had been unquestioning Confederates, some joined the Republicans for ulterior motives—whether out of pure political opportunism, belief that as Republicans they could better control black labor, or in an effort to coopt what looked certain to become the dominant party and steer it in a moderate direction—but others held strong Republican principles and still others exhibited varying combinations of both opportunistic and principled motivation.

There were indeed many Souths vying for supremacy during the tumultuous years after the Civil War; southern identity itself was up for grabs. Perhaps most significant, a diverse group of southerners now identified the South not with slavery, states' rights, and the Confederate rebellion, but with egalitarianism, progress, and opportunity. If some southerners had shown extraordinary enthusiasm for the Confederate experiment, others—in most of the South, at least as many—now showed similar enthusiasm for the *Reconstruction* experiment. (In some cases, the same people managed to be excited about both the Confederacy *and* Reconstruction.) This hidden South deserves emphasis because it would soon be submerged in the torrent of Lost Cause nostalgia that—as Gaines Foster, David W. Blight, and others have shown—did so much to foster the myth of a solitary, unified, unchanging South. Just as it is worth pointing out that a majority of southerners never supported the secession movement during the winter of 1860–61, so too it is noteworthy that a majority of southerners *did* endorse—by voting for Republicans—some version of Reconstruction between 1867 and 1870.[40]

Sarah W. Wiggins, *The Scalawag in Alabama Politics, 1865–1881* (University, Ala.: University of Alabama Press, 1977).

40. See Foner, *Reconstruction,* 314–33, 346–79. On the Lost Cause, see esp. Foster, *Ghosts of the Confederacy;* Roland G. Osterweis, *The Myth of the Lost Cause, 1865–1900*

—⁊⁊—

In short, southerners have disagreed over who is qualified to speak for the South and over what the South represents. In his travels through the South detailed in *Confederates in the Attic,* journalist Tony Horwitz repeatedly came upon southern whites who identified the Confederate flag—or, more precisely, the St. Andrew's Cross of the Confederate battle flag—as representing southern tradition and southern heritage: "I'm here today to stand up for heritage," one flag defender told him in South Carolina; "that's what the flag's all about." Typically, such defenders combined a visceral attachment to the flag as symbol of "their" past with insistence that the Confederacy was not simply about defending slavery, resentment against "political correctness," anger at being pushed around by "big" outside forces (especially the federal government), and unselfconscious appeals to white racism. Typical, too, were vague expressions of southern "peoplehood," such as historian Shelby Foote's assertion that he would have supported secession had he lived in 1861 because "I'd be with my people, right or wrong." "The way I see it," one Virginian told Horwitz, "they were fighting for their honor as men. They came from stock that was oppressed and they felt oppressed again by the government telling them how to live."[41]

(Hamden, Conn.: Archon Books, 1973); Charles Reagan Wilson, *Baptized in Blood: The Religion of the Lost Cause* (Athens: University of Georgia Press, 1980); Gary W. Gallagher and Alan T. Nolan, eds., *The Myth of the Lost Cause and Civil War History* (Bloomington: Indiana University Press, 2000); and Blight, *Race and Reunion,* especially 255–99.

41. Tony Horwitz, *Confederates in the Attic: Dispatches from the Unfinished Civil War* (New York: Pantheon Books, 1998), quotations: 80, 149, 35. For a good brief survey of contemporary southern efforts to define—and honor—Confederate "heritage," see Charles B. Dew, *Apostles of Disunion: Southern Secession Commissioners and the Causes of the Civil War* (Charlottesville: University Press of Virginia, 2001), 4–10. For an example of a spirited defense of southern "heritage" against "cultural cleansing," see the e-mail letter of anthropologist Virgil Huston to H-SOUTH@H-NET.MSU.EDU, 10 January 2000. "The national culture of the United States is violent and profane, coarse and rude, cynical and deviant, and repugnant to the Southern people and to every people with authentic Christian sensibilities," the Tuscaloosa, Alabama-based League of the South asserted in its "Declaration of Southern Cultural Independence"; *Wilmington* (Delaware) *News Journal,* 5 March 2000, A1. For the mixed appeal of Confederate symbols, with a continuum of "traditionalist" perspectives ranging from "a love of Southern history and values" to "an ideology of racism and intolerance," see J. Michael Martinez, "Traditionalist Perspectives on Confederate Symbols," in *Confederate Symbols in the Contemporary*

The prevalence of such views suggests a number of observations. Most obvious, it points both to the continuing immediacy of the Civil War for many white southerners today and to a powerful resentment that those southerners feel against a "big" federal government oblivious to the rights of "little" people, a resentment that is of course by no means uniquely southern. But it also raises a series of troubling questions about southern identity and self-consciousness at the turn of the twenty-first century. First of all, as numerous commentators have pointed out, if the Confederate flag represents southern "tradition," it is very much an invented or reinvented tradition, resurrected in the middle of the twentieth century during the Dixiecrat campaign of 1948 and the struggle against school desegregation in the 1950s and 1960s; the incorporation of the St. Andrew's Cross in Georgia's state flag occurred in 1956 and the Confederate flag's position atop the state capitol building in Columbia, South Carolina, dates from 1962. Less often raised, however, is a second (and I think more important) question that deserves attention: whether it is desirable for anyone, southerners or not, to identify blindly with their "heritage" or "tradition." If we are all shaped by the actions of those who came before us, including our ancestors, none of us is responsible for those actions. To what extent, then, should we be either proud or ashamed of the behavior of our ancestors—whether biological or metaphorical? Such identification (whether positive or negative) with attributes of one's birth over which one has no control—color, ethnicity, nationality, "heritage"—would seem on its face to be positively un-American, a flagrant rejection of the notion that we judge people on the basis of their behavior, character, and achievements, not their birth.[42]

South, ed. J. Michael Martinez, William D. Richardson, and Ron McNinch-Su (Gainesville: University Press of Florida, 2000), 243–83 (quotations: 244).

42. Originally the emblem of Robert E. Lee's Army of Northern Virginia, the Confederate battle flag became *the* Confederate flag only *after* the war, "over the course of the century between the 1860s and the 1960s"; see John M. Coski, "The Confederate Battle Flag in Historical Perspective," in Martinez, Richardson, and McNinch-Su, eds., *Confederate Symbols in the Contemporary South,* 89–129 (quotation: 89). On the continuing flag struggles in South Carolina and Georgia, see Robert Holmes and M. Christine Cagle, "The Great Debate: White Support for and Opposition to the Confederate Battle Flag," ibid., 281–302; and Ron McNinch-Su, William D. Richardson, and J. Michael Martinez, "Traditionalists Versus Reconstructionists: The Case of the Georgia State Flag, Part

But even more troubling is a third question: in identifying with the past, which past—and whose—are we adopting? Just as the Major-General in Gilbert and Sullivan's operetta *The Pirates of Penzance* acquires a new set of ancestors by purchasing a new estate—as he puts it, "I don't know whose ancestors they *were,* but I know whose ancestors they *are*"[43]—so too Americans, most of whom are not descendants of those who made the American Revolution, have acquired a revolutionary tradition. In that there have been many Souths, current-day southerners intent on celebrating their past must choose, on a continuing basis, *which* of these many Souths to embrace. The Reconstruction experiment was *also* part of the southern past, but those who talk of celebrating their heritage rarely seem interested in celebrating what W. E. B. Du Bois referred to as the "benefits" of Reconstruction; depending on one's perspective, one might suggest that Mississippi should celebrate having chosen the country's first black senator, Hiram Revels, in 1870, or that southerners in general should celebrate as the "liberation" of the South Robert E. Lee's surrender to Ulysses S. Grant at Appomattox. Certainly, *some* southerners would deem those events to be memorialized.[44]

One," ibid., 303–21. For the argument, based on multivariate analysis of 1994 polling data, that racial attitudes were preeminent in determining whether white Georgians supported or opposed changing the state flag, see Beth Reingold and Richard S. Wike, "Confederate Symbols, Southern Identity, and Racial Attitudes: The Case of the Georgia State Flag, Part Two," ibid., 322–35. The same was clearly true in Mississippi as well, where voters in a state referendum soundly rejected a proposal to remove the St. Andrew's Cross from the Mississippi state flag; see "Battle Lines Form Again on the Battle Flag," *New York Times,* 4 April 2001, A10, and "Mississippi Votes by Wide Margin to Keep Flag That Includes Confederate Emblem," *New York Times,* 18 April 2001, A12.

For a debate between Norman Podhoretz and Victor Navasky enunciating two competing notions of patriotism, one of which celebrates one's country as it is, "right or wrong," and the other of which sees a more principled love for one's country in celebrating its virtues while struggling to remedy its defects, see the *New York Times,* 1 July 2000, B7. In response to Podhoretz's distaste for "America-bashing," Navasky countered that "patriotism is best expressed in the struggle to make this a better place."

43. *The Complete Works of Gilbert and Sullivan* (New York: Modern Library, 1936), 163.

44. Du Bois, "Reconstruction and Its Benefits," *American Historical Review* 15 (July 1910): 781–99. For a recent collection that highlights the diverse ways in which various

The uses of the past are of course subject to continuing debate. Does one celebrate one's entire past, just because it exists? Can one learn from the mistakes—or, more than mistakes, evils—of the past? Is either a celebratory or a condemnatory approach to the past the most useful way for us to understand either its significance or our relationship to it? Clearly, the struggle over the past is also, in part, inevitably a struggle over the present. As David W. Blight put it in discussing the struggle over southern memory and identity, "those who can create the dominant historical narrative, those who can own the public memory, will achieve political and cultural power."[45]

Throughout the world, people are grappling with questions that once appeared self-evident, central among which are the salience, character, and utility of "nations." In many ways, the quest to come to grips with southern identity represents a similar problem, one rooted in making sense of the way in which those who live in particular geographical regions have developed self-consciousness as a people. Because this is such a pervasive issue in the modern world, it is one that is best approached in comparative context. In chapter 3, I shall turn my attention to what we can learn by comparing the South with what I call "other Souths," which of course need not actually be southern in a purely latitudinal sense.

---

groups of southerners remember the past—and how "controversies over what of the past should be remembered provide the crucible for future definitions of any meaningful southern identity"—see W. Fitzhugh Brundage, ed., *Where These Memories Grow: History, Memory, and Southern Identity* (Chapel Hill: University of North Carolina Press, 2000); the quotation is from Brundage's "Introduction: No Deed But Memory," 15. On the varied "legacies" that make up southern history, see also Edwards, *Scarlett Doesn't Live Here Anymore,* 189.

45. David W. Blight, "Epilogue: Southerners Don't Lie; They Just Remember Big," in Brundage, ed., *Where These Memories Grow,* 349. Raising the question of whether "the hidden memories" of "marginalized groups [can] be incorporated into the public life of the South," Brundage suggested that "in fact no 'common cultural canopy' exists in the South. To the extent that the memories of groups in the South diverge, they can share neither experiences nor assumptions." Brundage, "Introduction," ibid., 16.

3 OTHER SOUTHS

The third kind of comparison that I want to address, that between the South and regions outside the United States, is the kind that people identify most readily as comparative. As with North-South and internal southern comparisons, those between the South and "other souths" can focus either on whole societies or on specific features of those societies, such as slavery, family relations, or the course of industrialization; the second approach has been more prevalent than the first, although comparisons of specific features often yield broad societal implications. In either case, however, transnational studies have usually been more explicitly comparative than those focusing internally on the South, and some scholars, such as George Fredrickson, consider them the only real form of comparison.[1] Although I do not share this judgment, I regard this kind of comparison as especially fruitful. Of course, some may suspect that I am not entirely unbiased on this question.

What is "comparable"? In approaching this question, I would

1. Fredrickson proposes that the term "comparative history" be reserved for scholarship that "has *as its main objective* the systematic comparison of some process or institution in two or more societies that are not usually conjoined within one of the traditional geographical areas of historical specialization"; George M. Fredrickson, "Comparative History," in *The Past Before Us: Contemporary Historical Writings in the United States,* ed. Michael Kammen (Ithaca, N.Y.: Cornell University Press, 1980), 458. See also Fredrickson, "From Exceptionalism to Variability: Recent Developments in Cross-National Comparative History," *Journal of American History* 82 (September 1995): 587–604. On the importance of considering the American past in broad global perspective, see the essays in Thomas Bender, ed., *Rethinking American History in a Global Age* (Berkeley: University of California Press, 2002).

suggest that anything *can* be compared with something else, but that utility is the key to comparison's desirability. Historical comparison can serve at least three major functions. First, it can lead to a reduction of parochialism, through an awareness of alternatives and a clarification of significance. For example, historians have long known that the American slave population grew very rapidly, more than tripling between 1810 and 1860 even though legal importation of slaves ended in 1808, but the significance of this natural population growth became clear only when they realized that it did *not* occur in most other New World slave societies.[2] The utility of this kind of comparison rests in a comparative awareness that derives from juxtaposing the different demographic experiences of slaves in the United States and the rest of the Americas, rather than from rigorous comparative analysis.

The other two comparative functions require more systematic comparison as the historian seeks either to form generalizations, based on discovering common patterns, or to disprove a generalization or hypothesis by showing that in at least one case it is not accurate. These two functions, although apparently very different, in fact represent opposite sides of the same coin: through comparison, the scholar seeks to weigh the impact of specific historical conditions on the objects being compared, thereby distinguishing the particular from the general. Far from constituting a simple listing of similarities, successful comparison requires the existence of significant differences. The most useful comparisons are likely to involve either common items—such as labor systems, economic development, revolutions, families—in different historical environments, or apparently similar processes yielding very different results. In both cases, it is the interplay between similarities and differences that provides the comparison's utility.

The largest body of transnational comparative work on the American South has focused on the closely related topics of slavery and

2. For an early exploration of the significance of this now widely recognized contrast, see C. Vann Woodward, "Southern Slaves in the World of Thomas Malthus," in Woodward, *American Counterpoint: Slavery and Racism in the North-South Dialogue* (Boston: Little, Brown, 1971), 78–106.

race relations. Much of the early comparative literature appeared in direct response to a controversial book published in 1959, in which Stanley M. Elkins contrasted slavery in the southern United States with that in Latin America. Building on sociologist Frank Tannenbaum's argument that race relations in the United States were far more rigid than those in Latin America, Elkins shifted the focus to the severity of slave treatment, stressing what he considered the uniquely harsh conditions that prevailed in the American South. Because no Church or Crown existed in the South to limit the masters' arbitrary authority over their slaves, slavery there was a "closed system" in which "the dynamics of unopposed capitalism" reigned supreme; as a consequence, the slaves were the ultimate victims, reduced to a state of infantile dependence or, as Elkins termed them, "Sambos."[3]

During the 1960s and 1970s, at the same time that historians of the South demonstrated that most American slaves were far from Sambos, a largely different group of comparative historians challenged the notion of a uniquely harsh American slavery. Some of these scholars emphasized the extent to which—despite very different legal traditions—actual master-slave relations in the South had much in common with those in Latin America, while others argued that in purely material terms slavery in the South was *less* oppressive than that in Brazil and the Caribbean. The most telling (although by no means the only) evidence for this argument was the superior health enjoyed by American slaves, a point highlighted by their highly unusual natural population growth. But whether historians stressed common patterns or differences, most agreed that when one looked at how concrete historical conditions shaped actual slave relations, Elkins's interpretation did not hold up. This research also underscored the need to differentiate clearly between *slave treat-*

---

3. Frank Tannenbaum, *Slave and Citizen: The Negro in the Americas* (New York: Alfred A. Knopf, 1946); Stanley M. Elkins, *Slavery: A Problem in American Institutional and Intellectual Life*, 3[d] ed. (Chicago: University of Chicago Press, 1976), esp. 27–80 (quotations: 37, 82). For a specific study supporting Elkins's argument, see Herbert Klein, *Slavery in the Americas: A Comparative Study of Virginia and Cuba* (Chicago: University of Chicago Press, 1967).

ment and *race relations,* for if slave treatment in the United States was not unusually harsh, race relations there *were* unusually rigid, whether measured in terms of slaves' access to freedom or in terms of the extent to which whites distinguished among people of color rather than lumping them all together as "blacks."[4]

More recently, comparative historians of slavery have branched out in a variety of new directions. Although their work has lacked the common thematic approach evident earlier (in part because with the repudiation of the Elkins thesis, they also lacked a common target), comparisons in the 1980s and 1990s typically differed in focus from earlier efforts in at least three ways. Some historians shifted the

4. There is a vast literature from the 1970s focusing on slave agency in the antebellum South. Among the most noteworthy titles are John W. Blassingame, *The Slave Community: Plantation Life in the Antebellum South* (New York: Oxford University Press, 1972, and revised ed., 1979); Eugene D. Genovese, *Roll, Jordan, Roll: The World the Slaves Made* (New York: Pantheon, 1974); Herbert G. Gutman, *The Black Family in Slavery and Freedom, 1750–1925* (New York: Pantheon, 1976); and Lawrence W. Levine, *Black Culture and Black Consciousness: Afro-American Folk Thought from Slavery to Freedom* (New York: Oxford University Press, 1977). For a historiographical survey of this literature, see Peter Kolchin, "American Historians and Antebellum Southern Slavery, 1959–1984," in *A Master's Due: Essays in Honor of David Herbert Donald,* ed. William J. Cooper Jr., Michael F. Holt, and John McCardell (Baton Rouge: Louisiana State University Press, 1985), esp. 88–95.

Among the many comparative works from the 1960s and 1970s challenging Elkins's interpretation, see Marvin Harris, *Patterns of Race in the Americas* (New York: Walker, 1964), ch. 6; David Brion Davis, *The Problem of Slavery in Western Culture* (Ithaca, N.Y.: Cornell University Press, 1967), ch. 8; Eugene D. Genovese, "The Treatment of Slaves in Different Countries: Problems in the Application of the Comparative Method," in *Slavery in the New World: A Reader in Comparative History,* ed. Laura Foner and Eugene D. Genovese (Englewood Cliffs, N.J.: Prentice-Hall, 1969), 202–10; Eugene D. Genovese, *The World the Slaveholders Made: Two Essays in Interpretation* (New York: Pantheon, 1969), pt. I; Carl N. Degler, *Neither Black nor White: Slavery and Race Relations in Brazil and the United States* (New York: Macmillan, 1971); Woodward, "Southern Slaves in the World of Thomas Malthus"; and Richard S. Dunn, "A Tale of Two Plantations: Slave Life at Mesopotamia in Jamaica and Mount Airy in Virginia, 1799 to 1828," *William and Mary Quarterly* 34 (January 1977): 40–64. See Kolchin, "American Historians and Antebellum Southern Slavery," 102–11. More recent research on diet and height suggests that whereas antebellum slave *adults* were comparatively healthy, *children* were not; for a convenient summary, see Robert William Fogel, *Without Consent or Contract: The Rise and Fall of American Slavery* (New York: W. W. Norton, 1989), 123–47.

comparative lens from slave treatment to the slaves themselves, exploring such topics as slave resistance and slave economic activity.[5] Others expanded their geographical focus beyond the New World, including Africa and Eastern Europe as well as broad efforts at generalizing across time and space.[6] And still others began to explore the end of slavery—emancipation and its aftermath—in comparative perspective.[7] In short, despite significant interpretive disagreements,

5. Examinations of slave life include Peter Kolchin, "The Process of Confrontation: Patterns of Resistance to Bondage in Nineteenth-Century Russia and the United States," *Journal of Social History* 11 (Summer 1978): 457–90; Eugene D. Genovese, *From Rebellion to Revolution: Afro-American Slave Revolts in the Making of the New World* (Baton Rouge: Louisiana State University Press, 1979); Roderick A. McDonald, *The Economy and Material Culture of Slaves: Goods and Chattels on the Sugar Plantations of Jamaica and Louisiana* (Baton Rouge: Louisiana State University Press, 1993); Ira Berlin and Philip D. Morgan, "Labor and the Shaping of Slave Life in the Americas," in *Cultivation and Culture: Labor and the Shaping of Slave Life in the Americas,* ed. Ira Berlin and Philip D. Morgan (Charlottesville: University Press of Virginia, 1993), 1–45.

6. George M. Fredrickson, *White Supremacy: A Comparative Study in American and South African History* (New York: Oxford University Press, 1981), and *Black Liberation: A Comparative History of Black Ideologies in the United States and South Africa* (New York: Oxford University Press, 1995); Orlando Patterson, *Slavery and Social Death: A Comparative Study* (Cambridge, Mass.: Harvard University Press, 1982); Peter Kolchin, *Unfree Labor: American Slavery and Russian Serfdom* (Cambridge, Mass.: Harvard University Press, 1987); Shearer Davis Bowman, *Masters and Lords: Mid-Nineteenth Century U.S. Planters and Prussian Junkers* (New York: Oxford University Press, 1993); and the AHR Forum "Crossing Slavery's Boundaries," which includes David Brion Davis's article "Looking at Slavery from Broader Perspectives" and comments by Peter Kolchin, Rebecca J. Scott, and Stanley L. Engerman, *American Historical Review* 105 (April 2000): 451–84.

7. Stanley L. Engerman, "Economic Adjustments to Emancipation in the United States and British West Indies," *Journal of Interdisciplinary History* 13 (Autumn 1982): 191–220; Eric Foner, *Nothing But Freedom: Emancipation and Its Legacy* (Baton Rouge: Louisiana State University Press, 1983); Steven Hahn, "Class and State in Postemancipation Societies: Planters in Comparative Perspective," *American Historical Review* 95 (February 1990): 75–98; Peter Kolchin, "Some Thoughts on Emancipation in Comparative Perspective: Russia and the United States South," *Slavery and Abolition* 11 (December 1990): 351–67, and "Some Controversial Questions Concerning Nineteenth-Century Emancipation from Slavery and Serfdom," in *Serfdom and Slavery: Studies in Legal Bondage,* ed. Michael Bush (London: Longman, 1996), 42–67; Rebecca J. Scott, "Defining the Boundaries of Freedom in the World of Cane: Cuba, Brazil, and Louisiana After Emancipation," *American Historical Review* 99 (February 1994): 70–102; and Frederick Cooper, Thomas C. Holt, and Rebecca J. Scott, *Beyond Slavery: Explorations of Race,*

many scholars have recognized that southern slavery is best understood in the context of slavery and other forms of unfree labor elsewhere in the modern world.

Although no other branch of southern history has been subjected to such intensive comparative scrutiny as slavery, virtually every subject—from the status of women to religion, frontiers, and social structure—could benefit from an effort to put it in broader context. Some topics have already seen promising (although less than systematic) efforts at comparison.[8] In arguing that "climate has played a larger role in shaping southern distinctiveness than contemporary historians are prone to acknowledge," for example, A. Cash Koeniger bolstered his thesis with comparative analysis. Noting the widespread and persistent stereotype of southerners as "creatures of the heart" in contrast to northerners as "creatures of the head," he suggested that elsewhere too—in areas as different as California and France—"populations set off from their northern counterparts by warmer temperatures" have displayed "characteristics strikingly like those of the American South." Deploring the tendency to dismiss such arguments as "anachronistic curiosities," he noted that "south-

---

Labor, and Citizenship in Postemancipation Societies (Chapel Hill: University of North Carolina Press, 2000).

    8. For a variety of examples of promising efforts at comparison, see Kees Gispen, ed., *What Made the South Different?* (Jackson: University Press of Mississippi, 1990); Norbert Finzsch and Jürgen Martschukat, eds., *Different Restorations: Reconstruction and "Wiederaufbau" in Germany and the United States: 1865, 1945, and 1989* (Providence: Berghahn Books, 1996); Mark M. Smith, "Old South Time in Comparative Perspective," *American Historical Review* 101 (December 1996): 1432–69; Marc Egnal, *Divergent Paths: How Culture and Institutions Have Shaped North American Growth* (New York: Oxford University Press, 1996); and Camilla Townsend, *Tales of Two Cities: Race and Economic Culture in Early Republican North and South America: Guayaquil, Ecuador, and Baltimore, Maryland* (Austin: University of Texas Press, 2000). Building on C. Vann Woodward's observation that southerners, unlike northerners, have experienced military defeat, James C. Cobb has recently suggested that "the South's experience is . . . far more relevant to [i.e., similar to that of] the rest of the world than it is to that of the rest of our nation." Cobb, "Modernization and the Mind of the South," in his *Redefining Southern Culture: Mind and Identity in the Modern South* (Athens: University of Georgia Press, 1999), 209. See C. Vann Woodward, "The Irony of Southern History" (1953) in his *The Burden of Southern History* (New York: Vintage Books, 1961), 169–70.

erners of the era before air conditioning rarely doubted that climate shaped their lives." On a more general level, Jack P. Greene has examined the colonial-era South in the context of the larger Anglo-Atlantic world, in the process casting the question of southern distinctiveness in a new light. Pointing to substantial similarities among English settler societies in the Chesapeake, Lower South, Bermuda, the Bahamas, the Caribbean, and Ireland, Greene noted that it was Puritan New England that deviated "sharply from the mainstream of English development," whereas the Chesapeake experience was "normative"; in the colonial era, unlike the antebellum, southern distinctiveness was a non-question.[9]

As an inherently comparative question, southern economic "backwardness" has received some noteworthy comparative attention. Although measuring the economic performance of the South against that of the North has been the most common approach, using other economies as yardsticks can yield new insights. In disputing the thesis that slavery retarded southern economic development, for example, Robert W. Fogel and Stanley L. Engerman pointed out that if the South had been a separate country in 1860, it would have been the fourth richest in the world, behind only Australia, the North, and Great Britain. Roger L. Ransom and Richard Sutch used a similar comparative framework to make a very different point about the southern economy: debunking the notion that it was the Civil War that was responsible for the poverty that gripped the postbellum South, they noted that throughout history most other "war-devastated economies" have recovered relatively quickly and suggested, therefore, that "a closer examination of the asserted connection between the physical destruction and subsequent economic performance of the South seems in order." Other scholars,

9. A. Cash Koeniger, "Climate and Southern Distinctiveness," *Journal of Southern History* 54 (February 1988): 21–44 (quotations: 26, 24, 38, 30, 29); Jack P. Greene, *Pursuits of Happiness: The Social Development of Early Modern British Colonies and the Formation of American Culture* (Chapel Hill: University of North Carolina Press, 1988), 36, xiii. On the importance of air conditioning in reshaping the modern South, see Raymond Arsenault, "The End of the Long Hot Summer," *Journal of Southern History* 50 (November 1984): 597–628.

including Jonathan Wiener, Steven Hahn, and Barbara Fields, have debated the extent to which the postwar South followed the so-called "Prussian Road" to capitalism, a formulation originally developed by Lenin to distinguish an authoritarian (Prussian) model, in which landed elites retained their political hegemony by allying with industrial capitalists, from a democratic (American) model. And comparative works on planter elites by Shearer Davis Bowman and Enrico Dal Lago have yielded valuable insights on a range of hotly debated issues, from the relationship between the servile economies and capitalism to paternalism, class formation, and national identity.[10]

In recent years, there has been considerable interest in (and a number of conferences on) comparing the southern United States with southern Italy in order to explore the theme of regional distinctiveness. Despite obvious and important differences between the two regions, like the American South the Italian Mezzogiorno was traditionally perceived—both by contemporaries and subsequent scholars—as a "backward" region suffering from underdevelopment, poverty, and an absence of modernization in comparison with the North. Less urbanized, less industrialized, and less educated, the South was supposedly marked by "traditional" or "premodern" values, seigneurialism, a hierarchical social structure, conservatism, a

10. Robert William Fogel and Stanley L. Engerman, *Time on the Cross: The Economics of American Negro Slavery* (Boston: Little, Brown, 1974), 249–51; Roger L. Ransom and Richard Sutch, *One Kind of Freedom: The Economic Consequences of Emancipation* (Cambridge, Eng.: Cambridge University Press, 1977), 41; Jonathan M. Wiener, *Social Origins of the New South: Alabama, 1860–1885* (Baton Rouge: Louisiana State University Press, 1978), passim, esp. 71–73; Steven Hahn, "Emancipation and the Development of Capitalist Agriculture: The South in Comparative Perspective," in Gispen, ed., *What Made the South Different?*, 71–88, 166–71; Barbara Jeanne Fields, "The Advent of Capitalist Agriculture: The New South in a Bourgeois World," in *Essays on the Postbellum Southern Economy*, ed. Thavolia Glymph and John J. Kushma (College Station: Texas A&M University Press, 1985), esp. 84–89; V. I. Lenin, *The Development of Capitalism in Russia: The Process of the Formation of a Home Market for Large-Scale Industry* (1899; Moscow: Foreign Languages Publishing House, 1974), 32–33; Bowman, *Masters and Lords*; Enrico Dal Lago, *Southern Elites: American Planters and Southern Italian Noblemen, 1815–1865* (Baton Rouge: Louisiana State University Press, forthcoming).

propensity for violence, an exaltation of honor, and massive out-migration; well into the twentieth century, it appeared as a laggard desperately trying to catch up to the national norm.[11]

If both reality and self-serving stereotyping combined to frame perceptions of southern backwardness in Italy, as in the United States, it is noteworthy that in both countries historians have mounted challenges to the orthodox view that show some remarkable parallels even though they appeared independently of each other. Just as Fogel, Engerman, and their supporters insisted on the efficiency and dynamism of the southern slave economy, so did Marta Petrusewicz rebut the idea that the southern Italian *latifondo* was backward, feudal, and inefficient, stressing instead its flexibility and market-orientation. "For most of the nineteenth century," she maintained, "it remained a model of rationality." Meanwhile, other scholars stressed the diversity that existed in the Italian South—where there were also in effect many Souths—and questioned efforts to generalize about southern "character." Still other revisionists challenged the notion of unification constituting a decisive turning point—in some versions, a bourgeois revolution—in Italian history, just as their American counterparts raised similar questions about the impact of the Civil War. And in both countries, critics of revisionism responded by insisting that not all of the traditional stereotypes deserve to be abandoned ("in practice," as Lucy Riall put it,

11. On perceptions of the Italian South, see Gabriella Gribaudi, "Images of the South: The *Mezzogiorno* as Seen by Insiders and Outsiders," in *The New History of the Italian South: The Mezzogiorno Revisited,* ed. Robert Lumley and Jonathan Morris (Exeter, Eng.: University of Exeter Press, 1997), 83–113; John Dickie, "Stereotypes of the Italian South, 1860–1900," ibid., 114–47; and Martin Clark, "Sardinia: Cheese and Modernization," in *Italian Regionalism: History, Identity, and Politics,* ed. Carl Levy (Oxford, Eng.: Berg, 1996), 81–106. See also the papers presented at the Commonwealth Fund Conference on the Two Souths: Toward an Agenda for Comparative Study of the American South and the Italian Mezzogiorno (University College London, January 1999), many of which have been published in *The American South and the Italian Mezzogiorno: Essays in Comparative History,* ed. Enrico Dal Lago and Rick Halpern (Houndsmill, Eng.: Palgrave, 2002). For a stereotypical portrait of southern Italian backwardness, see Joseph Lopreato, *Peasants No More: Social Class and Social Change in an Underdeveloped Society* (San Francisco: Chandler Publishing Company, 1967). For a new comparative study, see Don H. Doyle, *Nations Divided: America, Italy, and the Southern Question* (Athens: University of Georgia Press, 2002).

the revisionist version of the Risorgimento "is hard to sustain"): the two Souths were indeed different in important ways from the rest of Italy and the United States, and the events of the 1860s did indeed constitute revolutionary transformations. The point is not, of course, that the Italian and American Souths were the same; Italy was not a slave society, and the United States does not have a history that stretches back more than two thousand years. Rather, the utility of the comparison stems from exploring specific subjects—regional identity, social structure, economic development—in settings that were partially similar and partially different, thereby providing a new context for familiar problems and encouraging new ways of thinking about those problems.[12]

Comparative analysis is equally promising in elucidating southern political history. Take, for example, the question of the basic conservatism that—despite some important exceptions, especially during the Reconstruction and Populist eras—has dominated southern politics from the antebellum period to the present. During the past forty years, as the Democratic Party abandoned its white supremacist tradition and came to champion a cautious expansion of federal power to promote greater racial and economic equality, that party lost the political hegemony it had held in the South during the first two-thirds of the twentieth century; meanwhile, the revamped Re-

12. Marta Petrusewicz, *Latifundium: Moral Economy and Material Life in a European Periphery,* transl. Judith C. Green (Ann Arbor: University of Michigan Press, 1996), 217 (quotation), and "Land Based Modernization and the Culture of Landed Estates in the Nineteenth-Century Mezzogiorno," in Dal Lago and Halpern, eds., *The American South and the Italian Mezzogiorno,* 95–111; Jonathan Morris, "Challenging Meridionalismo: Constructing a New History for Southern Italy," in Lumley and Morris, eds., *The New History of the Italian South,* 1–19; John A. Davis, "Changing Perspectives on Italy's Southern Problem," in Levy, ed., *Italian Regionalism,* 53–68; Lucy Riall, *The Italian Risorgimento: State, Society, and National Unification* (London: Routledge, 1994), esp. 51–59 (quotation: 65), and " 'Ill-Contrived, Badly Executed [and] . . . of no Avail'? Reform and Its Impact in the Sicilian *Latifondo* (c. 1770–1910)," in Dal Lago and Halpern, eds., *The American South and the Italian Mezzogiorno,* 132–52. In *Modern Italy: A Political History* (Ann Arbor: University of Michigan Press, 1997), Denis Mack Smith refers unapologetically to "the backward South" (432) in discussing the post–World War II era. For the debate over economic development in the *American* South, see above, chapter 1, pp. 25–29, and notes 25–30. For an innovative comparison of landed elites in the Italian and American Souths, see Dal Lago, *Southern Elites.*

publican Party, once the champion of civil rights but in its new incantation a bitter opponent of "big government" and federal interference in states' rights, gained ascendancy throughout much of the South. Equally striking was the racial polarization that accompanied this transformation: like African Americans elsewhere, black southerners came to vote overwhelmingly Democratic while white southerners voted almost as overwhelmingly Republican. As a result, the Democratic Party has become an endangered species in the increasingly white South, even as conservative Republicans have become a sectional staple as prevalent as cotton once was.[13]

Although this conservatism has usually been considered in a comparative context in which the South is contrasted with the North, southern politics can also be examined in light of regional politics elsewhere. In many European countries, politics has also been marked by regional patterns, although these patterns defy easy generalization. In England, the more prosperous South has voted consistently Conservative, while the North, suffering from the effects of deindustrialization and high unemployment, has shown strong pro-Labour proclivities. In Italy, by contrast, in a trend bearing some resemblance to that in the United States, the poorer South has tradi-

13. On the growing political conservatism and Republican hegemony in the contemporary South, see, inter alia, Earle Black and Merle Black, *Politics and Society in the South* (Cambridge, Mass.: Harvard University Press, 1987), *The Vital South: How Presidents Are Elected* (Cambridge, Mass.: Harvard University Press, 1992), and especially *The Rise of Southern Republicans* (Cambridge, Mass.: Harvard University Press, 2002); and Robert P. Steed and Laurence W. Moreland, "Southern Politics in Perspective," in *Confederate Symbols in the Contemporary South*, ed. J. Michael Martinez, William D. Richardson, and Ron McNinch-Su (Gainesville: University Press of Florida, 2000), 67–86. For background to this political realignment, see Kari Frederickson, *The Dixiecrat Revolt and the End of the Solid South, 1932–1968* (Chapel Hill: University of North Carolina Press, 2001). In 1996, southern whites voted for Bob Dole over Bill Clinton by 56 to 36 percent, while southern blacks voted for Clinton over Dole by 87 to 10 percent; in 2000, the racial disparity was greater still, with whites favoring George W. Bush over Al Gore by 66 to 31 percent and blacks choosing Gore over Bush by 92 to 7 percent. The gap is equally evident in voting for members of the House of Representatives: in 1996, southern whites voted Republican by 64 to 36 percent, while southern blacks voted Democratic by 85 to 15 percent; in 1998, whites voted Republican by 65 to 35 percent, while blacks voted Democratic by 89 to 11 percent. Voting statistics are from the *New York Times*, 10 November 1996, 28, 9 November 1998, A20, and 12 November 2000, Sect. 4, p. 4.

tionally shown less support than the rest of the country for parties of the left and more support for Church-affiliated parties pledged to defend traditional values. And in post–Cold War Germany, the East, after first indulging in a reflexive anti-Communist surge that provided the bulwark for Helmut Kohl's reelection to a third term as chancellor, expressed its disillusionment with the new order in 1998 by voting for candidates of the left, helping to bring about the replacement of Kohl's Christian Democrats by the current "Red-Green" coalition.[14]

But if regional voting patterns have existed elsewhere, they have been especially strong in the American South, not only because of that section's distinctive history but also because of the unusual weakness of the central government under the American federal system. Most other countries have countrywide school systems, drivers' licenses, and levels of unemployment compensation; in the United States, however, the augmented authority of states vis-à-vis the federal government makes possible an unusual degree of variation from the national political norm in regions where common interests, experiences, and values also deviate from the national norm. The South has been preeminently such a region.[15]

<hr>

14. For a regional breakdown, by party, of seats in British Parliament following the elections of 1974, 1979, 1983, and 1987, see J. Denis Derbyshire and Ian Derbyshire, *Politics in Britain from Callaghan to Thatcher* (n.p.: Chambers, 1988), 191. An Italian referendum of 1946 "showed 76 per cent at Naples and 85 per cent at Lecce in favor of retaining the monarchy, while the North voted heavily for a republic"; Smith, *Modern Italy*, 432. On the shift in East German voting patterns, see the *New York Times*, 28 September 1998, A10, and 29 September 1998, A1.

15. For emphasis on continued southern cultural distinctiveness in the post–World War II era, a distinctiveness rooted in "localism, violence, and a conservative religion," see, inter alia, John Shelton Reed, *The Enduring South: Subculture Persistence in Mass Society* (Lexington, Mass.: Lexington Books, 1976), quotation: 89; and Jeanne S. Hurlburt and William B. Bankston, "Cultural Distinctiveness in the Face of Structural Transformation: The 'New' Old South," in *The Rural South Since World War II*, ed. R. Douglas Hurt (Baton Rouge: Louisiana State University Press, 1998), 168–88. For varied judgments on this question, see the essays in Robert P. Steed, Lawrence W. Moreland, and Tod A. Baker, eds., *The Disappearing South? Studies in Regional Change and Continuity* (Tuscaloosa: University of Alabama Press, 1990). For the argument that the federal system played a vital role in promoting sectionalism in antebellum America, see Peter S. Onuf, "Federalism, Republicanism, and the Origins of American Sectionalism," in *All Over the*

—⁓—

Given the central importance of the Civil War to the very concept of the South, the section's Civil War experience must loom especially large in any comparative approach to southern history. Needless to say, the American version is hardly the only civil war in history; dozens of others, from the English Civil War of the 1640s to the conflict that has raged in the Congo on and off from the early 1960s to the present, invite comparison. A number of prominent historians, including Eric L. McKitrick, David M. Potter, and Carl N. Degler, have essayed such an approach, although none of these efforts has yet been especially successful in shaping Civil War historiography, and a systematic comparative study of the American Civil War still awaits its author. Perhaps the most influential example of comparison designed to shed light on American Civil War history has been McKitrick's imaginative but questionable use of the post–World War II behavior of the vanquished Axis powers to suggest that if the Confederates had accepted their defeat with more humility in 1865, they would have been spared the imposition of a vindictive Reconstruction settlement. In suggesting that the Germans and Japanese, by unconditionally repudiating their wartime goals, met the "symbolic needs" of the victors and thereby undercut anti-German and anti-Japanese sentiment among the Allies after the war, McKitrick skillfully emphasized the recalcitrant postwar behavior of the ex-Confederates; at the same time, however, he ignored the largely diplomatic reason for the absence of a "harsh" post–World War II reconstruction program—the imperatives of an emerging cold-war policy—as well as the very real persistence of bitter anti-German and anti-Japanese sentiment in the Allied countries that suffered most heavily in the war (especially the Soviet Union, Poland, China, and Korea).[16]

Map: Rethinking American Regions, ed. Edward L. Ayers et al. (Baltimore: Johns Hopkins University Press, 1996), 11–37. On growing centrifugal forces in Great Britain, as voters in Wales, Scotland, and Northern Ireland seek heightened autonomy, see, inter alia, "The United Kingdom's Overhaul," *New York Times,* 9 May 1999, Section 1, p. 14.

16. Eric L. McKitrick, *Andrew Johnson and Reconstruction* (Chicago: University of Chicago Press, 1960), 21–41. See also David M. Potter, "The Civil War in the History of the Modern World: A Comparative View," in his *The South and Sectional Conflict* (Baton

In approaching the Civil War comparatively, one can begin with the number of casualties. The Civil War was by far the bloodiest confrontation in the history of the United States, a point sensitively explored by Drew Gilpin Faust in her recent essay, "A Riddle of Death." The war resulted in about 620,000 deaths, or roughly 2 percent of the American population, and led to an even higher proportion—about 2.9 percent—of *southern* deaths. It is therefore worth emphasizing that when compared with other countries' military experiences, the American Civil War ranks as a midlevel conflict, one in which death and destruction were certainly widespread but of nowhere near record-breaking proportions. In the premodern era, wars (often in combination with deadly epidemics) could produce devastation on a scale rarely seen in the nineteenth or twentieth centuries; much of France and Germany, for example, suffered massive depopulation during the Hundred Years War (1337–1453) and the Thirty Years War (1618–48) respectively. Even in more recent times, however, mortality rates in the American Civil War were far from exceptional. Sudan, for example, has about the same number of people today that the United States had in the 1860s, but the civil war that has racked that African country for the past two decades has produced more than 2 million deaths, well over three times the number killed in the American conflict. And as a proportion of the population, the number of Soviets who perished in World War II was about five times as great as the number of Americans and three times as great as the number of southerners killed in the Civil War.[17]

Rouge: Louisiana State University Press, 1968), 287–99; and Carl N. Degler, "One Among Many: The Civil War in Comparative Perspective," 29th Annual Robert Fortenbaugh Memorial Lecture (Gettysburg: Gettysburg College, 1990).

17. Drew Gilpin Faust, " 'A Riddle of Death': Mortality and Meaning in the American Civil War," 34th Annual Robert Fortenbaugh Memorial Lecture (Gettysburg: Gettysburg College, 1995). See C. V. Wedgwood, *The Thirty Years War* (Garden City, N.Y.: Anchor Books, 1961), esp. 490–96, for a rough estimate that "the German Empire . . . probably numbered about twenty-one millions in 1618, and rather less than thirteen and a half millions in 1648" (quotation: 496). As of 1998, the Sudanese civil war had claimed about 6 percent of the population, including "one in five southern Sudanese"; *New York Times,* 12 December 1998, A6. Estimates of Soviet deaths in World War II are imprecise, but typically fall in the 20–25 million range; for a recent suggestion of 8.6 million Soviet soldiers and "at least 17 million civilians" killed in the war, see William C. Fuller, "The Great

An international context also provides a useful venue for returning to the question of southern national identity during the Civil War. The concepts of "nation" and "nationalism" have received considerable attention in recent years, in part because of the explosion of nationalist violence that has rocked much of the world and in part because of the collapse of competing methods of conceptualizing human relationships: in an era in which ideals of socialist solidarity and class consciousness seem to have lost much of their salience, national identity looms correspondingly larger as a way of explaining how people relate to each other. In exploring this subject, it is useful to begin with Benedict Anderson's idea of a nation as an "imagined community," that is, a body of humans whose shared sense of identity makes them seem to constitute a "people." Despite the common assumption that national identity, nationalism, and resulting national animosities are usually the products of centuries-old traditions, they appear in fact to be relatively recent developments in human history and to be more often imposed from the top down than reflections of immutable popular folkways. Rather than constituting natural phenomena, nations and a sense of nationality are *created*.[18]

Fatherland War and Late Stalinism, 1941–1953," in *Russia: A History,* ed. Gregory L. Freeze (Oxford: Oxford University Press, 1997), 319–46 (quotation: 334).

18. Benedict Anderson, *Imagined Communities: Reflections on the Origin and Spread of Nationalism,* 2ᵈ ed. (London: Verso, 1991); E. J. Hobsbawm and Terence Ranger, eds., *The Invention of Tradition* (Cambridge, Eng.: Cambridge University Press, 1983); E. J. Hobsbawm, *Nations and Nationalism Since 1780: Programme, Myth, Reality* (Cambridge, Eng.: Cambridge University Press, 1990); William Pfaff, *The Wrath of Nations: Civilization and the Furies of Nationalism* (New York: Simon and Schuster, 1993); and Patrick J. Geary, *The Myth of Nations: The Medieval Origins of Europe* (Princeton: Princeton University Press, 2002). It is important to distinguish *nation* from *state,* terms that are often confused in English but typically differentiated in central and eastern Europe (and their languages, as in "Volk" versus "Staat" in German and "narod" versus "gosudarstvo" in Russian); on this point, see Theodore R. Weeks, *Nation and State in Late Imperial Russia: Nationalism and Russification on the Western Frontier, 1863–1914* (DeKalb: Northern Illinois University Press, 1996), 4–8. See also Ernest Gellner, *Nationalism* (London: Weidenfeld & Nicolson, 1997). For a recent attempt to understand "nation" as both imagined community and product of collective memory, see Alon Confino, *The Nation as a Local Metaphor: Würtemberg, Imperial Germany, and National Memory, 1871–1918* (Chapel Hill: University of North Carolina Press, 1997).

Considering the creation of southern nationalism, and of the Confederate nation, in international context suggests some intriguing themes that so far as I know have not been explored. The very basis for Confederate identity is striking for its atypicality. Sense of nationhood in the modern world has usually been built around varying combinations of language, religion, and "ethnicity." Using these to create national identification occurred both in countries that were already in existence—as in nineteenth-century France, where much of the country did not speak French and local attachments were usually stronger than national—and in those where independence or unity was forged in "national" struggles, as in Italy, Germany, Poland, and Ireland. Rather than nations making states, argued E. J. Hobsbawm, "states . . . created 'nations.' . . . The Italian kingdom . . . did its best, with mixed success, to 'make Italians' through school and military service, after having 'made Italy.'" The spreading sense of Polishness or Irishness (or more recently Serb-ness and Croatian-ness) depended on accentuating differences reconfigured as longstanding and immutable: we have our *own* language, religion, traditions, folklore, and culture that have since time immemorial made us a people. It also depended on accentuating common elements that supposedly united a people at the expense of class (and other) differences that divided them: class consciousness and nationalism are historical enemies.[19]

Despite the best efforts of Confederate propagandists, linguistic, religious, and ethnic identification were of minimal use in creating Confederate nationalism; indeed, all three served to unite Confederates and Yankees rather than to divide them. Like many African "nations" today—nations that, based on the legacy of European colonial administration, lack linguistic, religious, or ethnic bases—the Confederacy faced both exceptional difficulties and tantalizing

19. E. J. Hobsbawm, *The Age of Empire: 1875–1914* (London: Weidenfeld and Nicolson, 1987), 150. For a recent overview of nationalism and conditions likely to breed it, see Michael Hechter, *Containing Nationalism* (Oxford, Eng.: Oxford University Press, 2000). Noting that in 1994, "eighteen of the twenty-three wars being fought were based on nationalist or ethnic challenges to states" (3), Hechter suggested that nationalism emerged most frequently under conditions of "direct rule," which "explains why nationalism is a creature of the last two centuries" (29).

opportunities in forging national consciousness. Loyalty to the new Confederate nation rested primarily on the defense of perceived interests, the foremost of which was slavery, and anyone committed to those interests qualified as a Confederate. As Vice President Alexander Stephens put it, the "great truth that the negro is not the equal to the white man; that slavery . . . is his natural and moral condition" constituted the "cornerstone" of the Confederacy. Perhaps nothing indicated the peculiarly inclusive nature of Confederate nationalism—and of the Confederate nation—more strikingly than the enthusiastic support that many members of the South's tiny Jewish community showed for the Confederate cause and the readiness with which such Jews found acceptance as good Confederates. At the heart of the effort to forge a slaveholders' republic, and of Confederate self-identification, was not a shared religion, language, or ethnicity but a shared ideological vision.[20]

In the ideological basis of its nation-building—although not in the ideology itself—the Confederacy resembled two other countries born in revolution: the United States and the Soviet Union. In both of these countries, national identity initially rested on a common

20. Stephens quoted in *The Civil War and Reconstruction: A Documentary Collection*, ed. William E. Gienapp (New York: W. W. Norton, 2001), 71–72. On the extent to which Confederate leaders and slaveowners saw the war as one for slavery, see Drew Gilpin Faust, *The Creation of Confederate Nationalism: Ideology and Identity in the Civil War South* (Baton Rouge: Louisiana State University Press, 1988), 59–60; and James L. Roark, *Masters Without Slaves: Southern Planters in the Civil War and Reconstruction* (New York: W. W. Norton, 1978), 1–32, 68–108. But see Faust's discussion of religion "as a source of legitimation for the Confederacy," in *The Creation of Confederate Nationalism*, 22–40 (quotation: 22); and Paul D. Escott's discussion, in *After Secession: Jefferson Davis and the Failure of Confederate Nationalism* (Baton Rouge: Louisiana State University Press, 1978), of how Jefferson Davis deliberately de-emphasized slavery in his public statements in order to win the allegiance of nonslaveholding whites. On Jewish support for and acceptance by the Confederacy, see Robert N. Rosen, *The Jewish Confederates* (Columbia: University of South Carolina Press, 2000). On similar enthusiasm for the Confederacy among Irish immigrants in the South—together with widespread "native tolerance" toward these overwhelmingly Catholic immigrants—see David T. Gleeson, *The Irish in the South, 1815–1877* (Chapel Hill: University of North Carolina Press, 2001), 141–72 (quotation: 194). On the problems involved in African "nation-building," see Basil Davidson, *The Black Man's Burden: Africa and the Curse of the Nation-State* (New York: Times Books, 1992).

commitment to an ideal, in one case to republicanism and in the other to socialism. Both were widely spoken of as "experiments" and received enthusiastic support elsewhere as beacons pointing the way to a better world. (And like the Confederacy, both aroused the bitter condemnation of those convinced that they pointed not to a better world but to disaster.) To "friends of liberty" and supporters of the "toiling masses," the United States of America and the Union of Soviet Socialist Republics were worthy of support and emulation because their identity rested on general principles rather than on a particular language, religion, or ethnicity. So too did the Confederacy's.[21]

In trying to create a sense of nationhood on the basis of shared ideology, all three countries faced unusual difficulties, for ideological enthusiasm is notoriously hard to sustain over prolonged periods. During World War II, when push came to shove, Soviet leaders played down socialism and appealed to old-fashioned Russian patriotism. More recently, of course, despite the once-apparent success of the Soviet Union in forging a sense of supernationality over three-quarters of a century, nationalist, ethnic, and religious loyalties have proven surprisingly resilient, even as the socialist ideal has collapsed. This is not the place to discuss how it occurred, but the successful creation of an *American* sense of nationality—which appeared gravely threatened in the Civil War—must stand as one of the world's most remarkable feats of nation-building.[22]

21. For a recent essay noting the ways in which nineteenth-century American nationalism departed from European models, and criticizing theorists of nationalism for ignoring the United States, see Peter J. Parish, "An Exception to Most of the Rules: What Made American Nationalism Different in the Mid-Nineteenth Century?" *Prologue: Quarterly of the National Archives* 27 (Fall 1995): 219–29. For the suggestion that perceived interest rather than shared culture lay at the heart of southern nationalism, see David M. Potter, "The Historian's Use of Nationalism and Vice Versa" (1963), reprinted in his *The South and Sectional Conflict*, 34–83.

22. On the "making" of an American nation—and nationalism—see David Waldstreicher, *In the Midst of Perpetual Fetes: The Making of American Nationalism, 1776–1820* (Chapel Hill: University of North Carolina Press, 1997). For a perceptive analysis of the tension between two conflicting strains of American nationalism—one "civic," rooted in the ideal of universal equality, and the other "racial," based on assumption of shared ethnicity—see Gary Gerstle, *American Crucible: Race and the Nation in the Twentieth Century* (Princeton: Princeton University Press, 2001). See also Eric Foner, *The Story of American Freedom* (New York: W. W. Norton, 1998), especially 37–45. Despite her recent

Viewed in this light, one can suggest that in the long run the architects of the Confederacy faced almost insuperable odds, not of a
military but of a political nature. In the Confederate case, all of the
problems associated with creating a new sense of ideologically
driven national identity were compounded by the nature of the ideology in question. Slavery—even when dressed up with appeals to
states' rights and honor—proved a poor cornerstone on which to
build national commitment at home or national support abroad. If
the American and Soviet experiments drew enthusiastic support
around the world from republicans and socialists, there were few
"friends of slavery" to rally to the Confederate cause. Within the
South, although I think that there is little evidence for the widespread "guilt" over slavery that some analysts have seen, slavery represented an *interest* (and a minority interest, at that) more than a
glorious cause that could serve to forge a new national consciousness. It is no wonder that after military defeat Confederate nationalism collapsed so quickly; after all, the abolition of slavery had
removed the most compelling basis for that nationalism. Despite
pride in their past and mythical delineations of the "Lost Cause,"
virtually no one in the South seriously proposed resurrecting the
Confederacy at some future date, or—as George M. Fredrickson has
noted—fighting on guerrilla-style, in the manner of the Afrikaner
nationalists in South Africa. Instead, the southern political elite immediately reversed course and began arguing that they were in fact
good Americans and that their states had never really been out of

---

assertion that the American experience was "more typical than atypical of how disparate,
local communities and social groups imagine themselves part of a national family," much
of Cecilia Elizabeth O'Leary's evidence and argument supports a different judgment.
Noting that "the growth of a unifying national culture in the United States proved to be
unusually slow" and that "the development of an American nationalism lacked many of
what Peter Parish refers to as the 'building blocks' that other nations relied on"—
including "ancient blood ties and a long history"—she outlined a highly atypical pattern
of American nation-building: "In contrast to the activist role played by the political-insti-
tutional agencies of governments as diverse as Argentina, Germany, France, and Japan,
the development of patriotic culture in the United States relied on the initiative of indi-
viduals, private businesses, and organized patriots. The government would not make a
significant intervention until World War I." O'Leary, *To Die For: The Paradox of American Patriotism* (Princeton: Princeton University Press, 1999), 5, 15, 14, 49.

the Union. In comparative context, the "creation of Confederate nationalism" appears a more problematical venture than many scholars have recognized. Indeed, although there is no way to prove such an assertion, I would suggest that had the Confederates been successful on the battlefield, it is unlikely that their independent republic would have survived as long as the Soviet Union.[23]

Comparison is also a useful tool in approaching the sequel to the Civil War: emancipation. Indeed, emancipation can be viewed as the quintessential southern experience, at the intersection of the South's two most important defining features—slavery and the Civil War. If emancipation gave meaning to the war, it was the war that shaped the particular contours of emancipation in the South, an interaction that is especially evident in comparative context.

One might begin by noting a general point: the unusual way in which slavery came to an end in the United States made possible a more radical postscript to slavery—Reconstruction—than was typical. Elsewhere in the modern Western world (with the exception of Haiti and the partial exception of Cuba), slavery ended peacefully. Although the masters sought to defend their privileges, they did not

23. George M. Fredrickson, "Why the Confederacy Did Not Fight a Guerrilla War After the Fall of Richmond: A Comparative View," 35th Annual Fortenbaugh Memorial Lecture (Gettysburg: Gettysburg College, 1996), 23. On the Lost Cause mythology, see Gaines M. Foster, *Ghosts of the Confederacy: Defeat, the Lost Cause, and the Emergence of the New South, 1865 to 1913* (New York: Oxford University Press, 1987); Gary W. Gallagher and Alan T. Nolan, eds., *The Myth of the Lost Cause and Civil War History* (Bloomington: Indiana University Press, 2000); and David W. Blight, *Race and Reunion: The Civil War in American Memory* (Cambridge, Mass.: Harvard University Press, 2001), esp. 255–99. For evidence of widespread attachment to the Confederate cause in the present-day South, see Tony Horwitz, *Confederates in the Attic: Dispatches from the Unfinished Civil War* (New York: Pantheon, 1998). A form of Soviet "Lost Cause" sentiment is evident in the recent (successful) effort to adopt the old Soviet anthem—minus the lyrics celebrating the construction of Communism—as Russia's new national anthem. "If we agree that the symbols of the preceding epochs, including the Soviet epoch, must not be used at all, we will have to admit that our mothers' and fathers' lives were useless and meaningless, that their lives were in vain," declared Russian President Vladimir V. Putin, in language strikingly parallel to that of southerners intent on celebrating their "heritage." "Neither in my head nor in my heart can I agree with this." *New York Times,* 6 December 2000, A1, A8.

oppose abolition by force of arms. American slaveowners were not only unusually militant in elaborating arguments on behalf of the Peculiar Institution; they were also unusually militant in taking up arms to defend their cause. The consequences of this slaveholders' rebellion were numerous, but one of the most important was the extent to which it accentuated the revolutionary nature of emancipation (and the radicalism of Reconstruction). Widely regarded throughout the North as traitors, slaveholders lost the moral authority and political power to help shape the course of the postwar Reconstruction settlement. In other countries, former masters played an important role in setting the terms of the new, post-emancipation order. They typically received some form of compensation for the loss of their human property, and they often directed a gradual process of emancipation, lasting years or even decades. In the American South, by contrast, emancipation was immediate and uncompensated, and the former masters were largely excluded from setting the rules for the new order. The former slaves, meanwhile, were the beneficiaries of a remarkable body of legislation that gave them unusual access to civil rights and political power. In short, because of the distinctive way slavery died in the South, there occurred an unusually sharp break with the past.[24]

A more specific kind of comparison is also instructive—and here, I draw from my ongoing research for a comparative study of emancipation of the American slaves and the Russian serfs. Although in addressing this topic here it possible to touch only on the tip of the proverbial iceberg while promising fuller treatment in a later work, for the rest of this chapter I would like to elaborate on three relatively simple points that result from this comparison; in each case, my aim in this book is to further our understanding of southern emancipation by considering it in a new context.

The first point has to do with a striking contrast in the *process* of emancipation in Russia and the southern United States—the way in

24. For elaboration of this point, see Peter Kolchin, "The Tragic Era? Interpreting Southern Reconstruction in Comparative Perspective," in *The Meaning of Freedom: Economics, Politics, and Culture After Slavery,* ed. Frank McGlynn and Seymour Drescher (Pittsburgh: University of Pittsburgh Press, 1992), esp. 294–97.

which freedom came to the slaves and serfs. Set within a general framework, this contrast illustrates the wide range in how emancipation was effected in the nineteenth century, with Russia and the United States South representing polar extremes and other societies located at various positions in between these extremes. From the perspective of the southern historian, this contrast highlights the particular nature of the southern emancipation experience, for in many ways it was that experience that was notable for its atypicality.[25]

A basic difference, from which many others sprang, was in the *vehicle* of emancipation. In the United States, a democratic government imposed emancipation by force of arms, after crushing a bloody rebellion designed to safeguard slaveholder interests; in Russia, an autocratic government introduced emancipation peacefully, over the ineffectual protests of a nobility that lacked the political independence to play more than an obstructionist role. Despite losing their serfs, Russian noblemen remained the pillar of the autocracy, played a major role in drafting and implementing the new order, and saw their interests well protected. Southern slaveowners, by contrast, as losers in the Great Rebellion, lost most of their political power (at least temporarily) and hence much of their ability to shape the emancipation settlement, which was imposed upon them.

Under these circumstances, it is not surprising that the *terms* of emancipation were in most respects far more favorable to the freedpeople in the South than in Russia, and far more solicitous of the former masters' well-being in Russia than in the South. There is little need for me to dwell at length on the nature of the southern emancipation settlement, which (despite the intensity of the strug-

25. For a brief general treatment of the Russian contrast, see Peter Kolchin, "After Serfdom: Russian Emancipation in Comparative Perspective," in *Terms of Labor: Slavery, Serfdom, and Free Labor,* ed. Stanley L. Engerman (Stanford: Stanford University Press, 1999), 87–115, 293–309. For English-language surveys of emancipation in Russia, see Daniel Field, *The End of Serfdom: Nobility and Bureaucracy in Russia, 1855–1861* (Cambridge, Mass.: Harvard University Press, 1976); Peter A. Zaionchkovskii, *The Abolition of Serfdom in Russia,* ed. and transl. from the 3ᵈ (1968) Russian edition by Susan Wobst (Gulf Breeze, Fla.: Academic International Press, 1978); and David Moon, *The Abolition of Serfdom in Russia, 1762–1902* (Harlow, Eng.: Longman, 2001).

gle over Reconstruction policy) was conceptually remarkably simple and can be easily summarized. Its essence—as set forth in legislation that included the Thirteenth, Fourteenth, and Fifteenth Amendments to the Constitution and the Reconstruction Acts of 1867—was to extend to the freed slaves the same rights and privileges as those enjoyed by other Americans, including (for men) the right to vote, and then to allow the freedpeople to fend for themselves in a competitive, individualistic, democratic society. The major exception to this dominant laissez-faire policy was, of course, the Freedmen's Bureau, but this was a small, underfunded agency whose sponsors perceived it as a temporary measure, not a permanent feature of the new order. Most of Reconstruction's architects agreed with their opponents that protective legislation for the freedpeople was inappropriate and that the true test of the African Americans' character would lie in their ability to do things on their own; Frederick Douglass expressed this quintessentially American view succinctly in 1862, in responding to the question, "What shall be done with the four million slaves if they are emancipated?" "Do nothing with them," he replied; "mind your business and let them mind theirs."[26]

The terms of emancipation in Russia require more elaboration—both because most American readers are less familiar with them and because those terms are extraordinarily complex and confusing, even to experts in the field. Although a full summary would require far more space than I have available, some highlights, based on a drastic simplification of an extremely complicated process, deserve attention.[27] Tsar Alexander II's decree of February 19, 1861, and the enormous body of legislation that accompanied it set in motion a gradual rather than sudden process of emancipation. Although serfs received their "personal freedom" immediately, they remained

26. Frederick Douglass quotation from *Douglass' Monthly,* January 1862, reprinted in *Frederick Douglass: The Narratives and Selected Writings,* ed. Michael Meyer (New York: Modern Library, 1984), 374. The best general overview of Reconstruction remains Eric Foner, *Reconstruction: America's Unfinished Revolution, 1863–1877* (New York: Harper & Row, 1988).

27. On the next three paragraphs, see, in addition to other sources cited, Kolchin, "After Serfdom," 88–95.

under the partially circumscribed authority of their former owners as "temporarily obligated" peasants. The status of these temporarily obligated peasants was defined separately on each landed estate by "statutory charters" composed by their former owners (or those owners' agents), under the supposedly watchful eye of "peace mediators," the Russian equivalent of Freedmen's Bureau officials. The government's guidelines for the charters varied considerably from one area to another, in order to take account of different conditions in three geographic zones, which were in turn subdivided into nine, eight, and twelve "localities." After a two-year transition period, temporarily obligated peasants began the tortuous route to becoming "peasant proprietors" through a process known as "redemption," whereby the peasants collectively paid for their land allotments—and thus in effect for their freedom—at inflated prices, with interest, over a forty-nine-year period; by 1870, about two-thirds of the serfs had *begun* this redemption process, but peasants struggled with their payments until 1907 when, as a result of an imperial manifesto issued in 1905 under mounting revolutionary pressure, all remaining redemption debt was canceled.

Setting these contrasting emancipation provisions side by side suggests that a well-informed observer in the 1860s would have judged the American plan, for all its inadequacies, more likely to succeed than the Russian, which seemed designed more to stymie than to fulfill the peasants' aspirations. Of course, many observers were less than well informed. Pennsylvania Congressman Thaddeus Stevens, for example, in his eagerness to confiscate southern plantations and distribute them to former slaves, pointed to the Russian model as a precedent and praised Tsar Alexander II as a "wise man" for giving land to the peasants.[28] In fact, however, the peasants were not *given* land but were forced to buy, on highly unfavorable terms, land that they had already been allotted as serfs. Equally unpromising, from the point of view of the peasants, was the continued he-

---

28. On Thaddeus Stevens and confiscation, see Eric Foner, "Thaddeus Stevens, Confiscation, and Reconstruction" (1974), reprinted in his *Politics and Ideology in the Age of the Civil War* (New York: Oxford University Press, 1980), 128–49, and *Nothing But Freedom*, 9 (quotation).

gemony of the nobles, who received generous compensation for the loss of their serfs, maintained a host of legally defined privileges that set them off from the peasants, and dominated the very implementation of the emancipation settlement. Consider, for example, two important institutions designed to smooth the transition to freedom. In the South, the Freedmen's Bureau was staffed primarily by Union army officers; in Russia, the peace mediators were all noblemen and almost all former serfholders.

Perhaps nothing indicates the gap between these two versions of emancipation so well as the contrast between the simplicity of the one and the complexity of the other. Although Congress's Reconstruction policy emerged only gradually, after lengthy political debates and numerous compromises, conceptually the Reconstruction legislation was very simple: extending equal rights to the former slaves, it was worded so as to define *general* principles that applied to everyone. Take, for example, the Fifteenth Amendment to the Constitution: "The right of citizens of the United States to vote shall not be denied or abridged by the United States or by any state on account of race, color, or previous condition of servitude." By contrast, the Russian emancipation legislation established a multiplicity of different privileges and obligations that applied differently to different groups (making distinctions both between peasants and others and among peasants themselves). It was also incredibly verbose and difficult to understand, consisting of hundreds of pages of densely written text divided into numerous acts, rules, appendices, and decrees. It is no wonder that an estate steward in Nizhnii Novgorod Province wrote to his employer several weeks after promulgation of the emancipation decree, "I have the manifesto and legislation on the peasants but so far it is hard for me to understand them clearly," or that in subsequent years the peasants would spend so much time trying to "interpret" the legislation correctly.[29]

29. Letter of P. P. Abramov in *Krest'ianskoe dvizhenie v Rossii v 1857–mae 1861 gg.: Sbornik dokumentov,* ed. S. B. Okun' (Moscow: Izdatel'stvo "Nauka," 1963), 408. For the full text of the emancipation legislation, see *Polnoe sobranie zakonov Rossiiskoi Imperii,* 2d series, 55 vols. (1825–1881), Vol. XXXVI (1861), no. 36,650 (Alexander's manifesto) and nos. 36,657–36,675; for a convenient collection of the most important provisions, see V. A. Fedorov, ed., *Padenie krepostnogo prava v Rossii: Dokumenty i materialy,* Vol. II: *"Polo-*

—ᴍ—

In light of these *contrasts* in the process and terms of emancipation, it is noteworthy that there were some significant *similarities* in the consequences of emancipation and in the overall course of developments in Russia and the South during the last third of the nineteenth century. (And here I come to my second basic point in this comparison.) Of course, given the enormous differences between these two societies, it is not surprising that common trends often manifested themselves very differently: although the freedpeople struggled with their former masters over the division of economic resources in both the South and Russia, for example, the ways in which they struggled reflected differing historical traditions and prevailing conditions. But the very existence of similar patterns of development in the face of starkly contrasting environments deserves attention and raises troubling questions about the impact of the process and terms of emancipation—and of Reconstruction itself—on subsequent events. For in the broadest sense, one might suggest that despite the radical contrasts between Russia and the South in general and in the way freedom came to the serfs and slaves in particular, in many ways an observer from one of these post-emancipation societies would have found the history of the other eerily familiar.[30]

---

zheniia 19 fevralia 1861 goda" i russkoe obshchestvo (Moscow: Izdatel'svto Moskovskogo universiteta, 1967), 7–63.

30. Generalizations in this and the next eight paragraphs are based on—in addition to sources specifically cited—extensive reading in primary and secondary materials on Russia and the South in the post-emancipation era. Among the most important of these materials for the South are Freedmen's Bureau papers, plantation records, and publications and correspondence of freedmen's aid societies; for Russia they include reports of government officials ranging from local peace mediators to the Minister of Internal Affairs, peasant petitions, materials on statutory charters and redemption agreements, and correspondence (especially among authorities and landowners) generated by peasant unrest. In both countries, there has been extensive publication of documentary materials. The most ambitious such project for the southern United States is the Freedom and Southern Society Project, which has so far published a total of five of ten anticipated volumes of emancipation-related materials; see Ira Berlin et al., eds., *Freedom: A Documentary History of Emancipation, 1861–1867* (Cambridge, Eng.: Cambridge University Press, 1985–), and, for a selection from the first four of these volumes, Ira Berlin et al., eds., *Free at Last: A Documentary History of Slavery, Freedom, and the Civil War* (New York:

In both Russia and the South, emancipation ushered in a plethora of changes, large and small, associated with the fundamental if halting transformation of economies based on coerced labor into those predicated on variants of free labor. For the slaves and serfs, the most momentous change was the growth in personal freedom that sharply reduced—although it did not eliminate—the arbitrary control to which they had once been subject. But the very availability of this personal freedom, and the uses to which the freedpeople put it as they struggled to secure the fruits of liberty, led in turn to a wide variety of other changes. To take two simple examples, in both Russia and the South the freedpeople associated education with their free status and eagerly sought to take advantage of new opportunities for schooling that typically came first from private sources before yielding to government sponsorship. And in both Russia and the South, emancipation profoundly affected family relations, although not in precisely the same manner. If both peasant and black families now enjoyed greater autonomy, this change was more momentous in the South than in Russia because slave families had suffered more outside interference than had those of serfs. Whereas emancipation bolstered black families, freeing them from the fear of forcible separation, it undermined the coherence of extended peasant families by giving their members greater freedom to break up such units and strike out on their own. Growing economic opportunities in cities also disrupted peasant families, as men seeking work disappeared from their villages for months or even years at a time and moralists lamented the corruption of traditional values by strange new ways.[31]

New Press, 1992). For Russia, see especially the Ministry of Internal Affairs reports in *Otmena krepostnogo prava: Doklady Ministerstva vnutrennikh del o provedenii krest'ianskoi reformy 1861–1862* (Moscow: Izdatel'stvo Akademii nauk SSSR, 1950); reports of special imperial emissaries sent to maintain order immediately following emancipation, in E. A. Morokhovets, ed., *Krest'ianskoe dvizhenie v 1861 godu posle otmeny krepostnogo prava* (Moscow: Izdatel'stvo Akademii nauk SSSR, 1949); and three volumes of a massive collection of documents on the "peasant movement": Okun', ed., *Krest'ianskoe dvizhenie v Rossii v 1857–mae 1861 gg.*; L. M. Ivanov, ed., *Krest'ianskoe dvizhenie v Rossii v 1861–1869 gg.: Sbornik dokumentov* (Moscow: Izdatel'stvo sotsial'no-ekonomicheskoi literatury, 1964); and P. A. Zaionchkovskii, ed., *Krest'ianskoe dvizhenie v Rossii v 1870–1880 gg.: Sbornik dokumentov* (Moscow: Izdatel'stvo "Nauka," 1968).

31. For early Ministry of Internal Affairs reports on peasant enthusiasm for education, see *Otmena krepostnogo prava*, 43, 77, 92, 99, 109, 114, 150, 169, 188. Two recent surveys

Other lives changed as well. In both countries, former masters struggled to overcome bitter humiliation, to preserve as many of their prerogatives as possible, and to adjust to new conditions. If the masters' humiliation was far greater in the South—Russian noblemen were not defeated in war and denounced as traitors—in its broadest contours the reaction was similar: they sought to distance themselves from their ungrateful charges. The shock to paternalistic pretensions was especially notable in the South, where slaveowners had typically interacted with their slaves more closely on a day-to-day basis than had Russian noblemen with their serfs, but in both Russia and the South former masters now determined that emancipation had "freed" them from their annoying laborers. The shift from "laborlords" to "landlords" entailed a sharp reduction in personal contact between planter and laborer, one manifestation of which was a marked increase in planter absenteeism. "Many planters have turned their stock, teams, and every facility for farming, over

---

of post-emancipation educational efforts in Russia are Ben Eklof, *Russian Peasant Schools: Officialdom, Village Culture, and Popular Pedagogy, 1861–1914* (Berkeley: University of California Press, 1986); and Jeffrey Brooks, *When Russia Learned to Read: Literacy and Popular Literature, 1861–1917* (Princeton: Princeton University Press, 1985). Virtually all studies of the southern freedpeople have stressed their enthusiasm for education. For my treatment of the subject in Alabama, see Peter Kolchin, *First Freedom: The Responses of Alabama's Blacks to Emancipation and Reconstruction* (Westport, Conn.: Greenwood Press, 1972), 79–106. On African American education in the South as a whole, see Robert C. Morris, *Reading, 'Riting, and Reconstruction: The Education of Freedmen in the South, 1861–1870* (Chicago: University of Chicago Press, 1981); and James D. Anderson, *The Education of Blacks in the South, 1860–1935* (Chapel Hill: University of North Carolina Press, 1988).

For a typical complaint about the harmful effects of family divisions among the post-emancipation Russian peasantry, see N., "O krest'ianskikh semeinykh razdelakh v Voronezhskoi gubernii," *Voronezhskii iubileinyi sbornik v pamiat' trekhsotletiia g. Voronezha* (Voronezh: Izd. Voronezhskim Gubernskim Statisticheskim Komitetom, 1886), 331–35; for a good examination of the subject, see Cathy A. Frierson, "Razdel: The Peasant Family Divided," *Russian Review* 46 (1987): 35–52. For the impact of peasant out-migration on family and village life, see Jeffrey Burds, *Peasant Dreams & Market Politics: Labor Migration and the Russian Village, 1861–1905* (Pittsburgh: University of Pittsburgh Press, 1998); and Barbara Alpern Engel, *Between the Fields and the City: Women, Work, and Family in Russia, 1861–1914* (Cambridge, Eng.: Cambridge University Press, 1994), 1–100. For a good documentary collection on family life among the southern freedpeople, see Ira Berlin and Leslie S. Rowland, eds., *Families and Freedom: A Documentary History of African-American Kinship in the Civil War Era* (New York: New Press, 1997). See also Kolchin, *First Freedom*, 56–78.

to the negroes," reported a newspaper correspondent in 1869 from Hale County in Alabama's blackbelt, "and only require an amount of toll for the care of their land, refusing to superintend, direct, or even, in some cases, to suggest as to their management." In Russia, meanwhile, noblemen—who under serfdom had already shown strong absenteeist inclinations—divorced themselves still further from peasant agriculture. The complaint of one nobleman from Smolensk Province in 1872 that "the gentry do not farm, they have abandoned the land, they don't live on their estates," reflected, in fact, the tendency of an increasing number to take advantage of rising land prices by selling or renting their land to peasant cultivators; between 1861 and 1905, the amount of land owned by the nobility decreased by about 40 percent.[32]

On a more general level, in both Russia and the South emancipation was associated with a fundamental restructuring of the social order—termed the Great Reforms in the one and Reconstruction in the other—designed to drag societies perceived as backward into the nineteenth century. (In this respect, the Russian experience was unusually close to the American: unlike most other post-emancipation societies, Russia experienced a real "reconstruction" of its own.) Driven in part by the freedpeople's struggle to maximize their social autonomy and get as far from their former servile dependence as possible and in part by new measures introduced by reform-minded governments, traditional societies underwent significant transformation. In the South, Reconstruction governments established public-

---

32. Quotations are from the *Mobile Daily Register*, 30 May 1869; and Cathy A. Frierson, transl. and ed., *Aleksandr Nikolaevich Engelgardt's Letters from the Country, 1872–1888* (New York: Oxford University Press, 1993), 38. On the decline of noble landownership and the growing "peasantization" of agriculture, see A. P. Korelin, *Dvorianstvo v poreformennoi Rossii 1861–1904 gg.: Sostav, chislennost', korporativnaia organizatsiia* (Moscow: Izdatel'stvo "Nauka," 1979), 54–68, 77–129, 270–76; Seymour Becker, *Nobility and Privilege in Late Imperial Russia* (DeKalb: Northern Illinois University Press, 1985), 31–43, 108–14, 171–74; and Teodor Shanin, *Russia as a "Developing Society": The Roots of Otherness: Russia's Turn of Century, Volume I* (New Haven: Yale University Press, 1986), esp. 136–56. The best work on planters' efforts to cope with the new order is Roark, *Masters Without Slaves*, 111–209; for the "laborlord to landlord" formulation, see Gavin Wright, *Old South, New South: Revolutions in the Southern Economy Since the Civil War* (New York: Basic Books, 1986), 17.

school systems, built railroads, and adopted state constitutions based on the revolutionary idea of equal civil and political rights for all men. Russia's Great Reforms included—in addition to the great emancipation itself—measures to modernize the army, overhaul the country's archaic judicial system, introduce *zemstvo* assemblies as new organs of local self-government, and extend emancipation to peasants owned by the tsar and the state (who did not benefit from the 1861 edict). It is no wonder that historians of both Russia and the South have written of a basic transformation of society to which they have attached a variety of terms from "modernization" and "democratization" to "revolution" and "transition to capitalism." Eric Foner's succinct observation on the renewed prevalence of "the term 'revolution' . . . as a way of describing the Civil War and Reconstruction" finds striking parallel in L. G. Zakharova's description of Russia's emancipation and ensuing reforms as "a momentous event, a 'revolution,' a 'turning point'" recognized as such by "the lawmakers themselves, their contemporaries, researchers, the classics of Russian literature, and the founders of Marxism."[33]

And yet, any examination of emancipation's aftermath in Russia and the South must point to continuity as well as change. Often, change and continuity were so intertwined as to make their disentanglement virtually impossible. Even as the freedpeople struggled to maximize their independence, for example, they often used their augmented freedom to defend traditional ways. The peasants defied liberal proponents of village rationalization and privatization by clinging to the *mir* or village commune, an organization that had exercised considerable authority under serfdom but that now—with the reduction in the power of noble landlords that came with emancipation—held a *strengthened* position in the countryside. African

---

33. Foner, *Reconstruction*, xxiv; and L. G. Zakharova, "Samoderzhavie, biurokratiia i reformy 60-kh godov XIX v. v Rossii," *Voprosy istorii* 1989 (no. 10): 3. For a recent collection of essays, see Ben Eklof, John Bushnell, and Larissa Zakharova, eds., *Russia's Great Reforms, 1855–1861* (Bloomington: Indiana University Press, 1994); and the slightly different Russian edition, *Velikie reformy v Rossii 1856–1874* (Moscow: Izdatel'stvo Moskovskogo universiteta, 1992). See also W. Bruce Lincoln, *The Great Reforms: Autocracy, Bureaucracy, and the Politics of Change in Imperial Russia* (DeKalb: Northern Illinois University Press, 1990).

Americans in the South showed a similar attachment to the "invisible church" that had flourished under slavery and now became visible, and they disappointed northern white missionaries who sought to convert them from their "superstitious" practices. As liberal reformers found to their dismay, the heightened freedom that came with emancipation could be used in ways that they had not imagined.[34]

And ultimately, despite all the new developments, the social structure in both Russia and the South proved remarkably resistant to change. Despite all the gains made by the freedpeople, a generation after emancipation the vast majority of peasants and blacks remained at the bottom of the economic hierarchy. Freedom had brought great rewards, but it had not ended the poverty, exploitation, and dependence that characterized the lives of blacks and peasants. Despite notable exceptions, most freedpeople still labored in the fields, as they or their parents had before emancipation, and as most other emancipated peoples continued to do as well. What is more, emancipation seemed to have settled less than either its proponents or its opponents had expected. Just as in Russia the "peasant question"—supposedly resolved once and for all by emancipation—was a subject of heated debate in the 1870s, 1880s,

34. There is a burgeoning literature—much of it Western—on the persistence of traditional ways among the post-emancipation Russian peasantry. For a sampling, see Christine D. Worobec, *Peasant Russia: Families and Community in the Post-Emancipation Period* (Princeton: Princeton University Press, 1991); and many of the essays in Esther Kingston-Mann and Timothy Mixter, eds., *Peasant Economy, Culture, and Politics of European Russia, 1800–1921* (Princeton: Princeton University Press, 1991). On the peasant commune, see V. A. Aleksandrov, *Sel'skaia obshchina v Rossii (XVII–nachalo XIX v.)* (Moscow: Izdatel'stvo "Nauka," 1976); and Boris Mironov, "The Russian Peasant Commune After the Reforms of the 1860s," transl. Gregory L. Freeze, *Slavic Review* 44 (Autumn 1985): 438–67. On the northern missionary effort in the postwar South, see, inter alia, Joe M. Richardson, *Christian Reconstruction: The American Missionary Association and Southern Blacks, 1861–1890* (Athens: University of Georgia Press, 1986); and Robert Francis Engs, *Educating the Disfranchised and Disinherited: Samuel Chapman Armstrong and Hampton Institute, 1839–1893* (Knoxville: University of Tennessee Press, 1999). On religious independence among the freedpeople, see Kolchin, *First Freedom*, 107–27; and William E. Montgomery, *Under Their Own Vine and Fig Tree: The African-American Church in the South, 1865–1900* (Baton Rouge: Louisiana State University Press, 1993).

and 1890s, so too in the South the position of African Americans remained at the top of the political agenda.[35]

If the freedpeople remained largely at the bottom a generation after emancipation, there are some intriguing parallels in how they got there. Indeed, one of the most striking similarities in patterns of post-emancipation development can be seen in the dynamic of reform activity followed by reaction that characterized both Russia and the South from the 1860s to the 1890s. The heady enthusiasm expressed not only by freedpeople but also by a wide variety of reformers convinced that the dawning of a bright new era was at hand soon gave way to disappointment, dismay, and disillusionment, as Reconstruction and the Great Reforms were followed by an era of reaction and retrenchment. In both countries, an increasing number of "informed" observers (including many former reformers) concluded that the reforms had gone too far, that the freedpeople were not fully ready to exercise the freedom they had received in a responsible manner, and that blacks and peasants needed more careful supervision. In Russia, as in the South, "reconstruction" can be said to have ended in the 1870s; the office of peace mediators was abolished in 1874. As in the South, the conservative backlash accelerated in the 1880s and 1890s as concern for order and authority supplanted interest in uplifting the oppressed; in the new environment, govern-

35. On the persistence of the "peasant question," and the continuing but unsuccessful effort to reform village life in the late nineteenth century, see George Yaney, *The Urge to Mobilize: Agrarian Reform in Russia, 1861–1930* (Urbana: University of Illinois Press, 1982); David A. J. Macey, *Government and Peasant in Russia, 1861–1906: The Prehistory of the Stolypin Reforms* (DeKalb: Northern Illinois University Press, 1987); Thomas S. Pearson, *Russian Officialdom in Crisis: Autocracy and Local Self-Government, 1861–1890* (Cambridge, Eng.: Cambridge University Press, 1989); and Francis William Wcislo, *Reforming Rural Russia: State, Local Society, and National Politics, 1855–1914* (Princeton: Princeton University Press, 1990). The proper place of blacks in the South remained a central issue in southern post-Reconstruction thought and politics. For a sampling of works on this subject, see Woodward, *The Strange Career of Jim Crow*, 31–110; Williamson, *The Crucible of Race*, 79–323; J. Morgan Kousser, *The Shaping of Southern Politics and the Establishment of the One-Party South, 1880–1910* (New Haven: Yale University Press, 1974); Michael Perman, *The Struggle for Mastery: Disfranchisement in the South, 1888–1908* (Chapel Hill: University of North Carolina Press, 2001); and Glenda Elizabeth Gilmore, *Gender and Jim Crow: Women and the Politics of White Supremacy in North Carolina, 1896–1920* (Chapel Hill: University of North Carolina Press, 1996).

ment action was more likely to be aimed at limiting than at promoting the freedpeople's rights. Indicative of this trend were two acts of 1889 and 1890, one creating a new office of "land captains" to maintain order in the countryside and the other sharply curtailing peasant participation in *zemstvo* assemblies.[36]

How such different emancipation *processes* can have yielded such similar emancipation *consequences* is a question deserving careful analysis. Here, I can only suggest that the explanation contains both general and specific components. At the general level, one can point out that in the dashing of their hopes and expectations, the experience of southern blacks and Russian peasants was typical rather than unusual; wherever serfdom and slavery were abolished in the nineteenth century, the sequel was one of exploitation, dependence, and poverty, not equality and prosperity. At the specific level, however, the southern and Russian experiences were not entirely typical: other emancipations did not usually lead to the kind of widespread effort to restructure the social order that existed in Reconstruction and the Great Reforms. Indeed, if dashed expectations constituted a common feature of post-emancipation societies, I would suggest that this process was particularly pronounced in Russia and the South precisely because of their sweeping efforts at social transformation. The two regions experienced not only unusually far-reaching reconstructions, but also—in correspondingly pronounced fashion—the downside associated with the unraveling of those reconstructions.[37]

---

36. I put forth the argument for parallel reconstructions followed by reactions in "Some Thoughts on Emancipation in Comparative Perspective," esp. 354–63. On the post-reconstruction reactions, see sources cited in note 35.

37. Kolchin, "Some Thoughts on Emancipation in Comparative Perspective," 363–66. On post-emancipation social and economic adjustments, and the general dashing of hopes, see W. Kloosterboer, *Involuntary Labour Since the Abolition of Slavery: A Survey of Compulsory Labour Throughout the World* (Leiden, Netherlands: E. J. Brill, 1960); P. C. Emmer, ed., *Colonialism and Migration: Indentured Labour Before and After Emancipation* (Dordrecht, Netherlands: Martinus Nijhoff, 1986); Engerman, "Economic Adjustments to Emancipation in the United States and British West Indies," esp. 196–203; David Brion Davis, *Slavery and Human Progress* (New York: Oxford University Press, 1984), esp. 221–26; and Thomas J. Holt, *The Problem of Freedom: Race, Labor, and Politics in Jamaica and Britain, 1832–1938* (Baltimore: Johns Hopkins University Press, 1992), 115–

In considering the results of emancipation from the perspective of a generation later, it is also worth noting an unfortunate coincidence: it was a cruel irony that emancipation in the southern United States and Russia occurred at the onset of a generation-long agricultural depression that embraced much of the Western world during the last third of the nineteenth century. Southern historians are of course familiar with the agricultural protest movements of the 1870s–1890s that culminated in the Populist crusade, but the broader point here is that this was not a good time to be a small-scale agricultural producer, whether a landowner or one of the many kinds of dependent laborers that sprouted up in the South and Russia. In fact, this was one of the most inauspicious times one can imagine to embark on the emancipation and uplifting of an overwhelmingly agricultural population. Without wanting to adopt a totally myopic view of the possibilities, one might nevertheless employ a bit of counterfactual history to imagine how different things might have been had emancipation coincided with a generation-long "golden era" in agriculture, when farm prices were high and it was relatively easy for marginal producers to achieve success.

My third point suggests some ways that the Russian comparison sheds light on the struggle for southern identity. In both Russia and the South, emancipation generated enormous excitement as regions previously identified largely with reaction now embarked on daring new social experiments. (This would not, of course, be the last time that such was the case.) Just as the Reconstruction South seemed to many Americans to be on the cutting edge of history, so too "progressive" Russians rejoiced that their country was not only joining "enlightened" Europe but in one giant leap taking her place at the forefront of civilization. For a brief moment, before disillusionment set in, revolutionary democrats reveled in Russia's transformation. "The Manifesto of February 19 has given the beginning of freedom

---

76. On the lack of equivalent reconstructions in most post-emancipation societies, see Foner, *Nothing But Freedom*, 8–38; Thomas J. Pressly, "Reconstruction in the Southern United States: A Comparative Perspective," *OAH Magazine of History* 4 (1989): 14–34; and Hahn, "Class and State in Postemancipation Societies."

to the Russian people," exulted radical publicist Nikolai Ogarev. His colleague Alexander Herzen agreed, proclaiming the tsar a "liberator" whose "name already stands higher than all of his predecessors" and publishing in his journal *The Bell* an enthusiastic letter from Italian revolutionary Giuseppi Garibaldi asserting that the tsar-liberator had "placed himself among the greatest benefactors of humanity."[38]

In many ways, the immediate post-emancipation situation in Russia seemed remarkably similar to that in the South, with the same kind of tripartite struggle under way among the freedpeople, their former owners, and those in the middle—government officials and reformers. Just as the Freedmen's Bureau mediated between various apparently irreconcilable visions put forth by ex-slaves and ex-masters, so too did the peace mediators play an intermediate role between peasants and noblemen, simultaneously striving to dampen "unrealistic" peasant expectations while making sure that landowners did not continue to treat them as human property; as among Freedmen's Bureau agents, the peace mediators ran the gamut from enthusiastic supporters to determined opponents of the freedpeople's rights (although their noble background in general rendered them less sympathetic to the freedpeople and more inclined to share the landowners' perspective than were most Freedmen's Bureau officials). And as in the South, so too in Russia the freedpeople faced a bitter struggle with their former owners over the nature of their new relationship, a struggle fueled by the freedpeople's conviction that they were being cheated out of the *real* freedom that was rightfully theirs. Possessing a strong sense of their right to the land, many peasants found it difficult to believe that they were not now to receive all the noble-owned land that they had been forced to cultivate. As they told one local official in Orenburg Province, "We do not recognize the [emancipation] manifesto of February 19 because the tsar promised us liberty, but now they force us to pay or work for land, and there can be no liberty without land."[39]

---

38. All three quotations are from *Kolokol* [*The Bell*] no. 96 (15 April 1861): 806; no. 95 (1 April 1861): 797; and no. 97 (1 May 1861): 813. (Pages of *Kolokol* numbered consecutively within each annual volume, in 11-volume reprint series, Moscow: Izdatel'stvo Akademii nauk SSSR, 1962–64.)

39. Report of Orenburg Province Governor G. S. Aksakov to Minister of Internal Affairs P. A. Valuev, on peasants of Subulak, 13 March 1862, in Ivanov, ed., *Krest'ianskoe dvizhenie v Rossii v 1861–1869 gg.*, 203. On the peace mediators, see Natalia F. Ust'iantseva,

But putting these struggles side by side reveals, for all their similarities, significant differences in the way they were manifested, and in the process helps to clarify the nature of the post-emancipation struggle over southern identity. Here, I will mention only four of these differences. First, the scope of confusion over the nature of the new order was vastly greater in Russia than in the South—both because the actual process of emancipation in Russia was so much more complicated and because peasants had long been convinced that the land was rightfully theirs. Adhering to "naïve monarchism"—the belief that the tsar was on their side but was constantly stymied by the greedy noblemen and corrupt officials who surrounded him—these peasants expected much of emancipation and inevitably received too little to satisfy them. It is hardly surprising, then, that they expressed intense displeasure with the terms of the emancipation settlement (which were in fact far from generous) and insisted that the edict and legislation needed to be "read properly," by people who knew how to interpret them. According to widely held rumors, there was another—*real*—emancipation decree (the "golden charter") that the tsar intended for them; in one variant that spread as landowners and peace mediators drafted statutory charters, peasants who resisted giving their approval to these charters would receive real freedom on February 19, 1863, exactly two years after the initial manifesto. Similar rumors spread in the late 1870s, this time that true freedom would come on February 19, 1881, twenty years after the initial manifesto.[40]

Such "misunderstandings" were hardly the result of lack of communication from above. Indeed, concerned about the potential for disorder, the Russian government went to extraordinary lengths—

"Accountable Only to God and the Senate: Peace Mediators and the Great Reforms" (transl. Ben Eklof), in Eklof et al., eds., *Russia's Great Reforms*, 161–80.

40. Peasant dissatisfaction with—and interpretation of—the terms of emancipation can be traced in numerous documents in, inter alia, *Otmena krepostnogo prava*; Okun', ed., *Krest'ianskoe dvizhenie v Rossii v 1857–mae 1861 gg.*; Ivanov, ed., *Krest'ianskoe dvizhenie v Rossii v 1861–1869 gg.*; and Zaionchkovskii, ed., *Krest'ianskoe dvizhenie v Rossii v 1870–1880 gg.* For a thoughtful essay on naïve monarchism, and the suggestion that at times it represented a clever ploy of peasants in dealing with hostile authorities, see Daniel Field, "The Myth of the Peasant," in Field, ed., *Rebels in the Name of the Tsar* (Boston: Unwin Hyman, 1976), 208–15.

especially for a government unused to explaining its actions to anyone—to deflate exaggerated expectations and inform peasants of the
terms of the new dispensation. These efforts included distributing
hundreds of thousands of copies of the emancipation manifesto and
accompanying legislation, enlisting the powerful Orthodox Church
to help refute "false rumors," and dispatching a specially appointed
imperial emissary to each province to oversee initial implementation
of the emancipation provisions. Despite such measures, however,
the gap between official Russia's understanding of emancipation and
that of the peasant masses continued to widen. Over and over, officials reported on the peasants' "widespread false expectations" that
were being fanned by "various ill-intentioned people."[41]

Indeed—and here is the second difference—Russia saw widespread rural disorders in the spring and summer of 1861 that dwarfed
whatever emancipation-generated violence occurred in the southern
United States, as well as continuing resistance over the next two
years to what peasants regarded as a fraudulent emancipation settlement. Although widespread use of military force and savage resort
to exemplary reprisals curtailed the most intense violence within a
few months, peasants continued to seize diverse opportunities to ex-
press their dissatisfaction with the version of emancipation being
foisted upon them. One of the most notable manifestations of this
dissatisfaction was their widespread refusal—despite enormous pressure—to approve the statutory charters defining their new status,
charters that according to the bizarre provisions of the emancipation
legislation had to be presented to the assembled peasants (or their
representatives) for approval, but could be implemented whether or
not the peasants consented to their terms. More than half the peasants refused to give their consent, sometimes presenting pointed explanations of their refusal to peace mediators and other officials.

---

41. The quotation is from the report of the Minister of Internal Affairs, 20 December
1861, *Otmena krepostnogo prava*, 91. On some of these government efforts to defuse potential disorder, see "Iz obzor deistvii Ministersvta vnutrennikh del po zemskomu otdelu
s 1 ianvaria 1861 po 19 fevralia 1863 g.," in M. Lur'e, ed., "Reforma 1861 g. i krest'ianskoe
dvizhenie," *Krasnyi arkhiv* 75, no. 2 (1936): 62–82; and Z. Gurskaia, ed., "Tserkov' i reforma 1861 g.," *Krasnyi arkhiv* 72, no. 5 (1935): 182–91. For the reports of the special emissaries, see Morohkovets, ed., *Krest'ianskoe dvizhenie v 1861 godu*.

When one mediator arrived at an estate in Voronezh Province, for example, he found that "the peasants . . . consider the statutory charter not only contrary to their expectations, but totally illegal and arbitrary"; a crowd of 150 peasants shouted "We do not want it, this will not be! We will not allow this!" and remained in a state of high agitation until the arrival two weeks later of the district police chief and a detachment of soldiers. Set in the context of these Russian developments, the emancipation process in the southern United States appears almost orderly.[42]

Third, the collective manner in which the peasants expressed their grievances and aspirations puts the behavior of the southern freedpeople in useful perspective. The collective resistance offered by peasant villagers evident in the example I just provided was no aberration. Time after time, officials who attempted to talk peasants into submission remarked on their group solidarity. When authorities tried to separate the assembled peasants on a large estate in Orel Province into separate groups, "all explained that they constituted one commune and would not be divided"; vigorously resisting efforts to separate their leaders, again "they all shouted out, 'we are all a commune.'" Such protests were in fact collectively organized by the *mir,* or village commune, and reflected the longstanding communal character of peasant life. Literally constituting the peasants' world (*mir* means "world" and "peace" as well as commune) the *mir* was a central feature of village life through which peasants

---

42. The quotation is from a report of peace mediator Astaf'ev to the governor of Voronezh, 23 October 1861, in *Krest'ianskoe dvizhenie Voronezhskoi gubernii (1861–1863 gg.): Dokumenty i materialy,* I (Voronezh: Izdatel'stvo Voronezhskogo universiteta, 1961), 49; see also report of district police chief Golovinskii, 3 November 1861, *ibid.,* 50. The immediate reaction to emancipation can be surveyed in I. Kuznetsov, ed., "Semdesiat piat' let nazad (19 fevralia 1861 g.)," *Krasnyi arkhiv,* 74, no. 1 (1936): 5–36; Okun', *Krest'ianskoe dvizhenie v Rossii v 1857–mae 1861 gg.*; and *Otmena krepostnogo prava.* For a running total of statutory charters as they were implemented and approved, see the Minister of Internal Affairs's reports in *Otmena krepostnogo prava*; as of 3 January 1863, when charters were in place covering more than two-thirds of the newly emancipated peasants, a slight majority of the charters were implemented without the signatures of peasant representatives, and—since opposition was most pronounced on the largest estates—58 percent of the peasants lived on estates where charters lacked such signatures. (See *Otmena krepostnogo prava,* 282.)

dealt with the outside world via their elected representatives and or-
dered their everyday existence by helping the needy in time of crisis,
determining who should be drafted to meet a village's quota of military recruits, and (in most of Russia) periodically reallocating land
allotments and obligations among peasants to prevent the emergence of sharp inequality among them. With emancipation, the authority of the *mir* actually increased, in part because of its official
recognition by the emancipation legislation and in part because of
the reduced influence of the landowning nobility; for example, the
mir now replaced serfholders in deciding whether, and under what
circumstances, peasants could leave their home villages. Russian
peasant life in the years after emancipation remained profoundly
communal.[43]

Nothing like the peasant commune existed among southern
blacks. I have questioned elsewhere the tendency of some historians
(especially during the 1970s) to exaggerate the cohesiveness and fe-
licity of the antebellum slave community, and I will not reenter that
particular controversy here except to note that this did not in any
way imply questioning the existence of *cooperative* behavior among
slaves, behavior that was clearly widespread. The story of emancipation's impact on African Americans' collective life remains to be
told. Some historians have argued that the freedpeople often
shunned growing staple crops for market in favor of a limited autarky based on communal rather than individual landholding, although most of their evidence comes from the Carolina and Georgia
lowcountry, where slave conditions had long been atypical of those

43. The quotation is from the report of Orel Province Governor N. V. Levashev to
the Minister of Internal Affairs, 19 May 1862, in Ivanov, ed., *Krest'ianskoe dvizhenie v
Rossii 1861–1869 gg.*, 208. On the collective nature of peasant protest under serfdom, see
Kolchin, *Unfree Labor*, esp. 269–78. On the commune under serfdom, see Aleksandrov,
Sel'skaia obshchina v Rossii; and Kolchin, *Unfree Labor*, esp. 201–206. For the emancipation legislation's provisions concerning the commune, see Fedorov, ed., *Padenie krepostnogo prava v Rossii*, 16–27. On the post-emancipation commune, see Mironov, "The
Russian Peasant Commune After the Reforms of the 1860s"; L. I. Kuchumova, "Sel'skaia
pozemel'naia obshchina evropeiskoi Rossii v 60–70-e gody XIX v.," *Istoricheskie zapiski*
106 (Moscow, 1981): 323–47; and A. N. Anfimov and P. N. Zyrianov, "Nekotorye cherty
evoliutsii russkoi krest'ianskoi obshchiny v poreformennyi period (1861–1914 gg.)," *Istor-
iia SSSR* 1980, no. 4: 24–41.

in the South as a whole. Elsewhere, emancipation permitted the open flourishing of the most powerful black communal organization—the "invisible church"—but also led to significant centrifugal as well as centripetal forces among the freedpeople; among the most noteworthy of these centrifugal forces was the break-up of the slave quarters and the disappearance of gang labor, both of which clearly acted to make black life less rather than more collective. In any case, the Russian example should serve as a reminder that as they explore the post-emancipation life of African Americans, historians need to be aware of the limits as well as the existence of their collective behavior.[44]

Fourth and finally, the Russian comparison helps clarify the significance of race—and racism—in the redefinition of identity in the post-emancipation South. It is now a commonplace that "race" is a subjective construct rather than an objective reality, and that racial categorization has varied over time and space. In eighteenth- and early-nineteenth-century Russia, peasants seemed as different from noblemen as did blacks from whites, and defenders of serfdom forged arguments that were essentially racial, maintaining that peasants were innately incapable of freedom. Still, racial thinking came more easily to white southerners than to Russians, and was both more prevalent and more persistent. If, in emancipation's wake, both southerners and Russians engaged in a giant debate over the meaning of freedom, the nature of their social order, and what it meant to be southern or Russian, they resolved the question of identity very differently. Blacks became—or in some ways remained—*invisible* southerners. In 1890 or 1960—as in 1860—the archetypal

44. Peter Kolchin, "Reevaluating the Antebellum Slave Community: A Comparative Perspective," *Journal of American History* 70 (December 1983): 579–601. On the freedpeople's post-emancipation preference for communal agriculture, especially in the lowcountry, see Edward Magdol, *A Right to the Land: Essays on the Freedmen's Community* (Westport, Conn.: Greenwood Press, 1976); Foner, *Nothing But Freedom*, 74–110; Julie Saville, *The Work of Reconstruction: From Slave to Wage Laborer in South Carolina, 1860–1870* (New York: Cambridge University Press, 1994), esp. 42–70. On longstanding distinctive patterns of work and life among lowcountry blacks, see esp. Philip D. Morgan, "Work and Culture: The Task System and the World of Lowcountry Blacks, 1770 to 1880," *William and Mary Quarterly* 39 (October 1982): 563–99.

southerner was white; congressional supporters of both the unsuccessful Force Bill (which would have enforced Reconstruction voting provisions) and of the successful Civil Rights Act were deemed enemies of the South, even though those measures were designed to protect people who were southerners. Such a conceptualization of peasants would have been impossible in Russia. Peasants formed the vast majority of the population; far from being invisible Russians, they were the personification of the Russian people or "nation" (*narod*). Whereas measures designed to protect blacks could be portrayed as "antisouthern," it was therefore inconceivable that measures designed to benefit the peasants could be labeled "anti-Russian"; such a designation would have seemed simply bizarre.[45]

In considering the freeing of the southern slaves in comparative perspective, the Russian story is useful on at least two different levels. As part of a general comparison of emancipation, it confirms the distinctive nature of the southern experience, an experience notable both for the unusual way in which freedom came and for the unusually strenuous Reconstruction effort to make freedom real. At the same time, as an object of comparison with emancipation in the South, that in Russia offers some specific features and suggests some specific conclusions that go beyond those evident in the general picture. In the coming of freedom—its vehicle, preparation, and terms—the Russian and southern versions of emancipation were as different as any major variants. The unfolding of their emancipations, however, showed unusual parallels, with Russia providing at least a partial exception to the widely noted lack of significant "re-

45. For an influential essay on the construction of race, see Barbara J. Fields, "Ideology and Race in American History," in *Region, Race, and Reconstruction: Essays in Honor of C. Vann Woodward,* ed. J. Morgan Kousser and James M. McPherson (New York: Oxford University Press, 1982), 143–77. On "racial" defenses of serfdom, see Kolchin, *Unfree Labor,* esp. 170–71. The Russian term *narod,* like the German *Volk,* connotes both nation and people; on the one hand the Russian *narod* represents "Russianness," but on the other it constitutes the *common* people in contrast to elite "society." For varying Russian images of post-emancipation peasants, see Cathy A. Frierson, *Peasant Icons: Representations of Rural People in Late Nineteenth-Century Russia* (New York: Oxford University Press, 1993).

constructions" in other post-emancipation societies. The Russian-southern comparison can prove especially fruitful in clarifying questions of race and identity, because unlike New World slavery, Russian serfdom lacked an overtly "racial" dimension; most of the owners and the owned shared the same ethnic, religious, and national background. Although many contemporary and subsequent observers saw one in racial and the other in class terms, the struggles between the freedpeople and their former owners in the South and Russia were part of a common story.

AFTERWORD

This book represents at once a set of analytical essays on southern history and an exercise in a particular kind of comparative history, one that focuses on a specific region in comparative perspective. Comparison can serve a variety of analytical functions, from forming generalizations to disproving hypotheses; at a more prosaic—and no doubt more common—level, however, comparison provides context, enabling us to make more reasoned judgments even when focusing on a single case. In a sense, this is what historians do all the time, for context is essential to all historical inquiry. Historical judgments are usually based, however, on implicit, unarticulated comparisons; indeed, almost every historical statement of significance is implicitly comparative. The assertion that conditions were hard during the Great Depression, for example, derives its meaning from an understood but unstated comparative framework: conditions were hard compared to earlier, or compared to elsewhere, or compared to what was desired. Terming the United States a "great power" in the twentieth century implies that it was more powerful than other countries, or more powerful than it had previously been.

Unarticulated comparative frameworks, however, frequently lead not to clarification but to confusion and historical disagreement; indeed, I would suggest that disagreements among scholars often rest more on the differing comparative frameworks that implicitly underlie their judgments than on differing understandings of what actually happened. Historians who argue over whether or not Reconstruction was "radical," for example, are likely to disagree less over the specific course of events than over the appropriate (implicit) comparative framework in which those events should be judged: compared to the desires of freedpeople and Radical Republicans— and to the values of most current historians—Reconstruction may have appeared distinctly nonradical, but compared to what had existed before the Civil War or to what occurred in many other post-emancipation societies, the changes that swept the postwar South were radical indeed. Because historical judgments are typically based on implicit, often unrecognized, comparisons, making the implicit explicit can help us make sense of those judgments, and of the issues behind them. In short, because comparison is something that historians do all the time, "comparative history" of the type I am promoting represents not so much a fundamentally new approach to the past as an effort to add precision and clarity—by adding context—to our interpretations of the past.

These three essays constitute not only an exercise in a particular kind of comparative history, but also a brief for this kind of history— both in general and with application to the United States South. They represent an effort to nudge southern history away from the provincialism that so long characterized its practice and toward the kind of global concerns that are already transforming it into one of the most innovative fields of historical research. Coming to grips with the South is impossible, I believe, without considering the innumerable internal variations—and contested versions—that have rendered generalization about one "South" so frustrating; at the same time, making sense of a composite South requires a consideration of what lies beyond its borders, both in the North and abroad. The three different comparative frameworks that I have put forth in this volume represent a modest but I hope fruitful effort to provide context to some of the "big" questions that have dominated the study of southern history.

If placing the South in a broadened context can yield insights into long-debated questions of southern history, I think that such a comparison has much to offer students of other societies as well. One reason that the South attracts so much interest is that it lends itself so well to the study of "big" historical questions—continuity versus change, slavery and freedom, the meaning of "race," the formation of national identity, the struggle between local or regional and centralized authority. Because these are issues that are central to the human experience, southern history properly conceived is of more than regional interest, and examining the South in comparative context promises to further our understanding of these big questions elsewhere as well. In short, southern history is regional history, but it is also American history and world history.

INDEX